The Chinese Path and the Chinese Dream

By Li Junru

D1722903

FOREIGN LANGUAGES PRESS

First Edition 2014

ISBN 978-7-119-08600-2

©Foreign Languages Press Co. Ltd, Beijing, China, 2014

Published by Foreign Languages Press Co. Ltd

24 Baiwanzhuang Road, Beijing 100037, China

http://www.flp.com.cn E-mail: flp@cipg.org.cn

Distributed by China International Book Trading Corporation

35 Chegongzhuang Xilu, Beijing 100044, China

P.O. Box 399, Beijing, China

Printed in the People's Republic of China

The Chinese Path and
the Chinese Dream

Contents

Preface:
Starting With the "Cautious
Mention of a 'China Model'"

It is well known that there was a discussion on the "China Model" among Chinese thinkers from 2008 to the 18th National Congress of the Communist Party of China (CPC) convened at the end of 2012.

The background of the discussion was that China's economy showed a good performance and attracted wide attention while other countries were challenged by the international financial crisis triggered by the U.S. subprime mortgage crisis in 2008. Prior to the discussion, Goldman Sachs had already proposed a "Beijing Consensus" different from the "Washington Consensus" by researching and evaluating China's economic development. After 2008 more and more people have paid attention to the "Beijing Consensus." As a result, being optimistic about China and discussing and researching the China model has become a hot topic among Chinese thinkers. The discussion is well-grounded and reasonable.

However, I stated we should "cautiously mention the 'China

model'" at the very beginning of the discussion, and, more importantly, I think we should make more effort to research the "Chinese path."

I remembered I challenged the idea of the "China model" put forward by others at the seminar on the issue of Chinese Path in 2008. At that time, I delivered an impromptu speech in a soft tone and only emphasized that we should "cautiously mention the China model." In my opinion, China was likely to eventually form a Chinese development model entirely different from Soviet model because it launched large-scale, extensive and profound reform. However, it was still too early to mention the issue. Therefore, I made the following statement at the seminar, "Now many people are talking about the 'China model,' indicating our experience has attracted attention from and been valued by others. That's a good thing. It is an encouragement for our exploration as well as an education for those people who blindly look back nostalgically or blindly worship the West. However, we should be keenly aware in the course of research that our system has not taken full shape yet and that we need to continue our exploration in a scientific way. Mention of a 'model' which takes full shape does not meet the facts and is very dangerous. Why is it dangerous? On the one hand we may become self-contented and blindly optimistic, and on the other hand we may change the direction of reform. The target of our reform is the old system.

If we state that 'China model' has already taken shape when the old system is not entirely reformed and the new system is not improved and finalized, we are likely to change the target of reform into such 'model' and regard it as the target of the reform."

"The path of socialism with Chinese characteristics is a road of constant development and improvement. After long-term explorations and in particular the explorations over the last three decades since the introduction of the reform and opening-up policy on the path of socialism with Chinese characteristics, we have formed good development thinking, systems and mechanisms. However, we have not yet finished the task, and our system has not taken full shape. Therefore, in my opinion, we should properly summarize our experience and profoundly research the path. We should research problems that we encounter in practice, keep improving our development mode, system and mechanism, and constantly develop a path that brings hope to the Chinese people."

I also stated, "We should attach importance to two points when summarizing the Party's governing experience. Firstly, we should keep pace with the times and keep abreast of the progress of the development of the times. We will be eliminated by the progressive trend of history if we fail to do so. Secondly, we should act according to our abilities and be realistic and pragmatic. We should develop China as quickly as possible, but we should be aware of our strength and seek truth from facts. China has made historic progress and remarkable achievements in the course of more than 30 years of reform and opening-up, but we should bear in mind that China is still in the primary stage of socialism and lags behind more than 100 countries in per capita GDP. We should be proud of our achievements and at the same time be mindful of potential danger and take action within our capabilities when discussing the 'Chinese Path'. Hence I would rather say that it is a road that is being constantly developed and improved."

Therefore, I summarized my speech by "It is better to mention the 'China model' with caution."

At that time, I gave two reasons why we should do so. Firstly, we have not yet finished the reform and improved and finalized the system, so we should not be self-contented and blindly optimistic. Secondly, we should prevent the direction of reform from being shifted from reform of the old system to "reform" of the reform. I didn't say many things that I wanted to say so as to avoid misunderstanding by others. For example, I disapprove of "modeling" the practices of relying on the government's administrative measures and intensifying macro control when coping with the international financial crisis. In my opinion, we can take some special measures in special periods, but we can't normalize such measures and call such practices the "China model." I made such statements at relevant Chinese People's Political Consultative Conferences (CPPCC). I said so because history tells us we should be confident but not arrogant about our cause and we will make a mistake if we are hotheaded. We must remain cool-minded, and be keenly aware of modesty after achieving a great victory in reform and opening-up. I strongly support the statements emphasized by the CPC Central Committee that all the comrades in the Party must keep in mind their historic missions, remain modest and prudent, guard against arrogance and rashness, and maintain the style of plain living and hard struggle. We should be eager to make changes and innovations, and guard against rigid thinking and stagnation. We should not vacillate, relax our efforts or act recklessly. And we should never be intimidated by risks or confused by distractions. We must unswervingly forge ahead along the path of socialism with Chinese characteristics and work ever-harder to unite with and lead the people of all ethnic groups in China in working for a happy life and the bright future of the Chinese nation.

Unexpectedly, the *Beijing Daily* published my impromptu speech, which raised many echoes. Later the *Study Times* of the Party School of the CPC Central Committee summarized and published the views of Zhao Qizheng, me and other comrades which exerted an even greater influence. As a result, debates arose one after another. I believe debate is a good thing, as it at least can activate the academic atmosphere and evoke more thoughts. At that time, the leaders of the People's Publishing House and Social Sciences Academic Press hoped I would write a book about this for them to publish. I was touched, and thought of the name of the book—*Researching the Chinese Path*. Later, I laid the work aside because I was busy, and discussions on the issue gradually faded.

In April 2012 an editor of the People's Publishing House asked me to write a book titled, *Researching the Path of Socialism with Chinese Characteristics*. I promised to do so. Of course I did not talk about the "China model" in the book, but focused on the "path of socialism with Chinese characteristics," as we know that a correct path is crucial.

"The revolutionary party is the guide of the people and any revolution for which the party leads a wrong way is doomed to fail," said Mao Zedong[1]. This view was evidenced by the new democratic revolution in China, the history of the country after the founding of New China in 1949, as well as the great practice of socialist modernization since the adoption of the reform and opening-up policy.

I think the real value of our innovations in practices and theories since the reform and opening-up is that we have found the path of socialism with Chinese characteristics. In contemporary China, we will really adhere to socialism if we follow the path of socialism with Chinese characteristics.

On June 24, 2013 several leaders and editors of the Foreign Languages Press asked me to write a book *The Chinese Path and the Chinese Dream* for foreigners who want to know more about Chinese. I promised with pleasure for two reasons: First, I had already written *Researching the Path of Socialism with Chinese Characteristics* and thus had laid a solid foundation for the new book; second, there have been many new ideas about this since the 18th CPC National Congress, so I felt that it was necessary to write a new book.

I should note that I have no objection to researching a "China model" nor to comprehensive discussion on the history and main characteristics of a "China model" at a right time under the circumstances of richer practices and more mature conditions. However, we should first research and expound the "Chinese Path," because this path is dynamic in practice while the model is gradually formed in the course of development of the path.

This is the theme and origin of this book.

Overview: The Past, Present and Future of the Chinese Path

On May 5, 2011 I gave a speech titled, "The Past, Present and Future of the Chinese Path" at the China-EU Seminar on Future Development. The speech was written for international exchanges and was of course the result of my theoretical research, but it also reflects and summarizes my life experience and feelings.

I said our seminar was designed to discuss the "future" at that time. Maybe the topic was thought up by a young man because generally speaking young people look forward to the future, middle-aged people value reality and elderly people relish the past. My topic was "The Past, Present and Future of the Chinese Path," which may suit the interests of the young, middle-aged and elderly people.

My Little Grandson's Question

I told a story before starting my speech. I said that when we were watching the wedding of Prince William a few days previously my little grandson asked me: "Why does Britain have a queen?" He asked this question because China had no emperor for over a century, and all modern Chinese people regard emperors and queens as ancient monarchs.

I thought of the political systems and development roads of all the countries in the world when I answered the question.

The governing party and administrators in Britain take turns, but the royal family exists permanently; the head of state, governing party and administrators also take turns in France; the head of state, governing party and administrators remain almost unchanged for decades in some states; the governing party remains unchanged and party and state leaders take turns with age limit on tenure in China. Such differences in political systems highlight the difference between the "Chinese Path" and the paths of other states on which our discussion of the "Chinese Path" today is grounded.

History of the Chinese Path

The "Chinese Path" I mean is the "path of socialism with Chinese characteristics," which has been found by us in circuitous explorations by reflecting on the lessons of the Soviet model and summarizing our historical experience.

I say circuitous explorations because the Chinese people found this path after two explorations.

The first exploration began in 1956, when CPC leader Mao Zedong found Soviet practice did not completely accord with the actual conditions in China and saw the disadvantages of the Soviet model. He proposed at that time that we should explore a path of socialism that met the actual conditions in China by taking the Soviet experience as a mirror. Sadly, Mao Zedong failed to persist in the exploration, and made many mistakes. But he also left us much precious ideological wealth, provided valuable experience, made theoretical preparations and laid a material foundation for our later exploration.

As a result, China began the second exploration soon after the end of the "cultural revolution," i.e., the reform and opening-up introduced at the Third Plenary Session of the 11th CPC Central Committee at the end of 1978. In 1982, Deng Xiaoping, chief designer of China's reform and opening-up, inherited the cause unfinished by and precious wealth left by Mao Zedong, and proposed that "we should go our own way and build socialism with Chinese characteristics" by summarizing the historical experience of socialist construction in China and other countries. Since then, China has unremittingly explored this path and made remarkable achievements in the face of profound and complicated changes in both the domestic and international situations.

This is the origin and background of the "Chinese path" that is being discussed by many people around the world.

In the 21st century, Chinese society shows many characteristics of a new stage, and China stands at a new historical starting point of reform and opening-up. China is making new efforts while following its unique development road.

In other words, we focus on advancing exploration in the following three aspects while continuing to take economic development as our central task and concentrate on development.

First, we must follow a scientific outlook on development that puts people first and seeks comprehensive, balanced and sustainable development, accelerate the transformation of the economic development pattern and address difficulties in the way of China's balanced economic development and all-inclusive development to realize a sustained and sound development of the Chinese economy.

Second, we must focus on ensuring and improving the people's well-being, promote social development, innovate in the social management system, address difficulties in China's social transformation and strike a balance between economic and social development.

Third, we must focus on strengthening the Party's governance capacity, advanced nature and purity, develop intra-Party democracy, keep Party-people relations close, intensify efforts in combating corruption and upholding integrity, address difficulties in Party building, and improve the governance and exercise of power for the people.

Meanwhile, China unswervingly follows the path of peaceful development, firmly pursues the opening strategy of mutual benefit and undertakes more international responsibilities in global governance within its capability.

We notice in this development process that since the introduction of the reform and opening-up, Deng Xiaoping, Jiang Zemin, Hu Jintao and Xi Jinping have passed the relay baton to one another to unswervingly reform, develop and stabilize China on the path of socialism with Chinese characteristics regardless of difficulties. This way of keeping political continuity and keeping abreast of the times represent the advantages of Chinese politics and the unique features of the "Chinese path."

Where Is the Chinese Path Heading?

I have spent much time introducing the past and present of the "Chinese Path" for the purpose of expounding on its future.

I can't predict the future of China but I can analyze it according to signs in today's China. China's future is promising and encouraging based on my observations.

First, China must continue to follow the "Chinese Path" in the future. China will learn and draw on the experience of modernization of foreign countries based on its basic national conditions, which is the most important principle summarized by China in long-term explorations. China follows this path in the primary stage of socialism and will continue to follow it after the primary stage of socialism. In other words, China will not take the path of Western countries in economy, politics, culture, and social and ecological construction. Of course neither will it return to the old paths of planned economy and concentration of power politics. The "Chinese Path" is a new and correct path based on China's actual conditions. Moreover, this path has been found and opened up by more than a billion Chinese people by hard work and has witnessed good results. Consequently, the Chinese people will naturally cherish this path and unwearyingly follow it.

Second, China must continue to adhere to reform and opening-up. This is the most significant characteristic of the "Chinese Path" as well as the root reason, or fundamental driving force, why the "Chinese Path" has been constantly advanced. We have not yet finished the reform and our system is not yet finalized and mature. According to Deng Xiaoping's plan and requirements, China will basically establish mature systems of reform in all aspects by 2020. Now we have some successful experience in developing a socialist market economy and are reforming and improving systems in other aspects. We still have a long way to go, but will enjoy a promising future. The 18th CPC National Congress put forward that we should fully implement the overall plan for promoting economic, political, cultural, social and ecological progress, build a moderately prosperous society in all respects and deepen reform and opening-up in an all-around way, which constitute a great chapter in the reform. China's future lies in constantly deepening reform and opening-up.

Third, China already has directions and goals for its future. The "Chinese Path" already tells us that the goal of China's development and reform is to turn China into a modern socialist country that is prosperous, strong, democratic, culturally advanced and harmonious. Many people know the Chinese people share a characteristic of having long-term and short-term goals. China has already set the clear goals to complete the building of a moderately prosperous society in all respects by 2020 and basically realize socialist modernization by 2050. After the 18th CPC National Congress, Xi Jinping, newly elected CPC General Secretary and state president, connects such goals with the Chinese people's efforts over the past 100 years to rejuvenate the nation, thus forming extensive public opinion and a powerful force for the people of all ethnic groups to struggle for the "Chinese Dream." Therefore, China's future is predictable, existing in the goal of the Chinese people and their targeted struggle.

Meanwhile, the "Chinese Path" is neither a path of external expansion and invasion nor a path of world hegemony, but a development road on which China seeks development by winning a peaceful international environment, and safeguarding and promoting world peace through its development. In this sense, the future of China is a future of peaceful development.

In short, the path of socialism with Chinese characteristics running through China's past, present and future is a "Chinese Path" characterized by profound ideological connotation and rich scientific content.

"Path" in the Eyes of the Chinese People

Translation of "Path" and Interpretation of "Tao" in Chinese Culture

Cultural Discussion on the Significance of "Path"

Path: A Concept of Chinese Culture

Anyone who wants to know Chinese politics needs to know, understand and get familiar with China's political terms. "The path of surrounding the cities from the countryside and finally seizing national power" and "the path of socialism with Chinese characteristics" are the most typical Chinese political terms.

▋ "Path" in the Eyes of the Chinese People

All people who are familiar with China's modern and contemporary history know that the CPC has always attached great importance to the path or road it takes.

The CPC suffered losses in its early years from intra-Party dogmatism and following arbitrary commands by the Communist International. Mao Zedong proceeded from reality to find the path of surrounding the cities from the countryside and finally seizing national power, which was different from the path of the October Revolution led by Lenin, and eventually won the Chinese revolution. Since the introduction of the policies of reform and opening-up, China has accomplished remarkable achievements in economic and social development by following the path of socialism with Chinese characteristics proposed by Deng Xiaoping. Therefore, the CPC frequently states in its authoritative documents: "The issue of what path we take is of vital importance for the survival of the Party, the future of China, the destiny of the Chinese nation, and the well-being of the people."[2]

The title of the *Report to the 18th CPC National Congress* is "Firmly March on the Path of Socialism with Chinese Characteristics and Strive to Complete the Building of a Moderately Prosperous Society in All Respects."[3]

Therefore, to understand Chinese politics, it is necessary to first know the position of "path" in the eyes of the Chinese people.

Translation of "Path" and Interpretation of "Tao" in Chinese Culture

The "Chinese Path" we mean is the path of socialism with Chinese characteristics. *Taolu*, pronounced *daolu* in Chinese, is generally translated as path or road and sometimes as way in English.

Generally speaking, such translations are acceptable. However, they can also be discussed from the perspective of culture because both path and road fail to accurately reflect the profound meaning of "*Taolu*" in Chinese, which is composed of two Chinese characters, namely *tao* and *lu* (path or road), meaning path or road in line with the Tao.[4]

Tao was proposed by the outstanding Chinese thinker Lao Tse.

Tao is the core concept of Lao Tse's philosophic thinking, or Taoism.

Later, the Confucians, represented by Confucius and thinkers of other schools, accepted the concept of Tao and gave it their own understanding and interpretation. Therefore, Tao exerts a far-reaching influence and enjoys a very important position in Chinese philosophy and culture.

Tao has profound connotations in the Chinese culture and has become a synonym for the origin or general law of the universe featuring the unity of Heaven and Man.

Thinkers before Lao Tse identified Heaven as the origin of all things on Earth and didn't discuss whether Heaven had an origin or not. Lao Tse began to inquire into the origin of Heaven, and proposed Tao. "There was something undefined and complete, coming into existence before Heaven and Earth. How still it was and formless, standing alone, and undergoing no change, reaching everywhere and in no danger [of being exhausted]! It may be regarded as the Mother of all things. I do not know its name, and I give it the designation of the Tao." (Chapter 25, *Lao Tse*) In other words, he believed the Tao gave birth to all things on Earth.

After giving birth to all things on Earth, the Tao exists in all things as evidence for their existence, and becomes the universal law for the ceaseless self-improvement and development of all things. Such a law objectively exists, is invisible and inaudible, and needs to be experienced and known in practice, evidenced by the saying that "The Way that can be told of is not the Unvarying Way."

This profound thought of Lao Tse tells us two very important principles. First, we must act by following laws instead of doing whatever we want in the world. Second, as the understanding of law is a long-term process of exploration, we must be progressive, forever remain modest and prudent.

In 2012, I wrote the following in the preface to the *Proceeding from the New Historical Starting Point – On Scientific Outlook on Development* by Li Junru, published by the Shanghai People's Publishing House: "The Way that can be told of is not the Unvarying Way." The Tao is a concept that has the most profound connotation in Chinese culture characterized by "unity of Heaven and Man." The Tao indicates path, principle and morality. As an ancient saying goes, "A man of noble character studies to understand the Tao and save the world." I once said, "We must understand the Tao to rejuvenate China." Our innovations in practice and theory must be based on "understanding the Tao." I have studied the ideological history of the sinicization of Marxism as well as Mao Zedong thought and the theoretical system of socialism with Chinese characteristics including the Scientific Outlook on Development for the purpose of exploring the "Tao" of revitalizing the Chinese nation.[5]

I also stated why we must explore a path meeting the Tao: People may take an old or new path, an evil or right path. The most difficult task for a man is to dare to take a correct path and grasp the correct direction.

Contemporary China is a hopeful and promising starting point for some people, an eternal puzzle for some and an inexplicable fear for others. Hope, mystery and fear come from various interpretations of the rapid development of China as well as from a variety of understandings of political direction in contemporary China. I hope people will be confident in hope, replace mystery with exploration and leave fear to history.

Qu Yuan, a famous intellectual in ancient China, said, "Long as the way is I will keep on searching above and below." He showed a spirit of unremitting and persistent exploration on the issue of path.

Therefore, "path" or "road" is a concept of Chinese culture.[6]

Cultural Discussion on the Significance of "Path"

Knowing the cultural significance of "path" helps us to discuss the "Chinese Path." First, when discussing the "Chinese Path," we can't judge issues in China based on paths taken or values and systems established by other countries. Second, we can't be anxious to summarize Chinese practice and experience in a rigid way, because such summarization is likely to result in ossification.

We must analyze the inherent development laws and requirements of Chinese society, and study whether the paths taken by China accords with the "Tao," and how to continue to improve and develop the path of turning China into a country of socialist modernization that is prosperous, strong, democratic, culturally advanced and harmonious amidst the explorations of "path" by adhering to a spirit of exploration and objectively reviewing and summarizing China's history, reality, theories and practices, including experiences and lessons.

Similarly, to strive for the "Chinese Dream" of national rejuvenation, we must also study Chinese path and the path that meets the "Tao". After the 18th CPC National Congress, General Secretary Xi Jinping not only proposed that "To realize the great rejuvenation of the Chinese nation is the greatest dream of the Chinese nation since modern times,"[7] but also emphasized that "we must take the Chinese path to realize the Chinese Dream, that is the path of socialism with Chinese characteristics."[8]

"The Chinese nation is very creative. We created the great Chinese civilization, and we can continue to expand and embark on the development road that is suitable for China's national conditions. The people of all ethnic groups must strengthen their self-confidence in theory, path and system of socialism with Chinese characteristics, and firmly embark on the correct Chinese path."[9]

Opening of the Chinese Path:
History and Logic

How was the path of socialism with Chinese characteristics opened? We can trace this question back to the "cultural revolution" (1966-1976) and to clarifying confusion and bringing things back to order and comprehensive reform after the 10 years of chaos.

Historical Choice after the "Cultural Revolution"

The chaotic "cultural revolution", of no revolutionary significance, plunged the Party and the country into a very difficult situation and confused people's thoughts. Should China after the "cultural revolution" continue to take the old path of "taking class struggle as the key link" or the mistaken path of bourgeois liberalization, or blaze a new path that meets China's actual conditions and promotes socialist development? The Party and the Chinese people faced a historical choice of direction.

At this critical historical juncture, senior revolutionists of the Party, represented by Deng Xiaoping, boldly stood up and led the whole Party to clear up the confusion and bring things back to order by starting from the Party's path marked by the Third Plenary Session of the 11th Central Committee of the Communist Party of China convened at the end of 1978. First, we broke the mental slavery of the "Two Whatevers" (resolutely upholding whatever policy decisions Chairman Mao made, and unswervingly following whatever instructions Chairman Mao gave), led and supported the great discussion on the criterion of truth, and reestablished the Party's fact-based ideological line. Second, we resolutely abandoned "taking class struggle as the key link," realized the strategic shift of the key emphasis in the Party's work from class struggle to economic development, proposed that we should adhere to the Four Cardinal Principles[10]and the reform and opening-up policies, and formed the basic line (the Party's political line in the primary stage of socialism). Third, we boldly and resolutely redressed cases in which people had been unjustly, falsely or wrongly charged or sentenced, liberated a large number of veteran revolutionaries, put forward the requirement of "revolutionary, young, knowledge-based and professional officials" and formed the organizational line that met the needs of socialist modernization. On this basis, focusing on correctly evaluating Mao Zedong and the historical position of Mao Zedong thought, the Party adopted the Decision of the Central Committee of the Communist Party of China on Several Historical Issues Since the Founding of New China at the Sixth Plenary Session of the 11th Central Committee of the Communist Party of China.

The Party's second-generation central collective leadership with Deng Xiaoping at the core formed at the Third Plenary Session of the 11th Central Committee of the Communist Party of

China made a historical decision of reform and opening-up after leading the Party to shift the key emphasis of its work, opening the new period of socialist modernization and blazing the path of socialism with Chinese characteristics.

Starting Point of Practice and Characteristics of History

How did we explore and open the path of socialism with Chinese characteristics in practice?

History tells us the exploration led by Deng Xiaoping had two starting points. First, implementing reform of the household contract responsibility system in rural areas and setting up the four special economic zones of Shenzhen, Zhuhai, Shantou and Xiamen.

We used to place more emphasis on reform of the household contract responsibility system in rural areas than setting up the four special economic zones for the following reasons: China has a vast rural area and huge rural population; agriculture as the foundation of industry and the national economy made great contributions under the planned economic system and faced many constraints; China's backward economy and culture were mainly seen in the rural areas and entailed widespread poverty.

Therefore, rural reform concerned the whole situation and exerted a far-reaching influence.

However, as China's original rural economy failed to completely cast off small-scale production of the natural economy and semi-natural economy, the productive forces emancipated by reform in the rural areas were not yet completely modern social productive forces. To realize modernization, China had to modernize the productive forces, including strategic economic restructuring. Such modern productive forces could be gradually achieved by independent innovation and arduous struggle and be realized by referring to, leveraging and absorbing the advanced technologies, management methods and experience of foreign countries. Deng Xiaoping pointed it out in October 1978: "We must regard introducing international advanced technology and equipment as the starting point of our development.[11] I think we should adhere to the great policy of making use of foreign investment." [12]

As a result, a new way of thinking about development was proposed, namely to build Chinese socialism while opening widely to the outside world. The innovative significance and historical contribution of this thinking have just been fully realized now, but at that time many people thought it was only a supplementary means of China's modernization. Deng Xiaoping's thinking was first embodied by the establishment of the four special economic zones. The CPC Central Committee and the State Council agreed to set up special export zones in Shenzhen, Zhuhai, Shantou and Xiamen in July 1979, and decided to change the four special export zones into special economic zones in May 1980. Deng Xiaoping regarded these special economic zones as "windows" of technology, management, knowledge and foreign policy to understand the world as well as a "base" for modern economic development and talent training. Practice has proved the experiment of setting up special economic zones was successful.

Therefore, from the perspective of experimenting in the exploration process of Deng Xiaoping, like the implementation of the household contract responsibility system, the establishment of the four special economic zones was also the starting point for blazing the trail to socialism with Chinese characteristics and creating socialist theory with Chinese characteristics.

The two starting points of exploring socialism with Chinese characteristics under the leadership of Deng Xiaoping were the starting points of practice, and thus influenced the whole process of building socialism with Chinese characteristics and formed two historical characteristics of socialism with Chinese characteristics in its development process:

First, promoting reform of the economic system and other aspects and building socialism with Chinese characteristics based on China's realities. We have noticed that seeking truth from facts and proceeding from reality, as emphasized by Deng Xiaoping, are based on the basic national conditions of China in the primary stage of socialism. In other words, we must admit that China lags behind other countries and can't make the mistake of rushing for quick results again. However, we admit our backwardness because we want to change the backward state instead of doggedly keeping it. Therefore, Deng Xiaoping proposed that we must proceed from China's realities and must reform and seek development. The practice of the household contract responsibility system is based on China's reality as well as reform and development. Based on the process and experience of the formation and development of socialism with Chinese characteristics, we must first realize that proceeding from China's reality to promote reform of the economic system and other aspects and building socialism with Chinese characteristics are important historical features of this great practice.

Second, independently building socialism with Chinese characteristics in the course of integration into economic globalization. After the establishment of the four special economic zones, we successively opened up 14 coastal cities, set up economic open zones in the Yangtze River Delta, Pearl River Delta, Southeast Fujian Province and Bohai Sea Region, turned Hainan Province into a special economic zone, developed and opened Pudong in Shanghai, and set up the Shanghai Free Trade Zone, embarking on the new path of building socialism while opening up step by step. We came to see in practice that reform and opening up are correlated and promote each other. In particular, in the process of opening wider to the outside world, we are increasingly aware of the necessity of developing a socialist market economy, and thereby creating favorable conditions for improving the level of opening-up.

In particular, Deng Xiaoping made the important decision of opening-up to the outside world because it was needed by our modernization. He keenly grasped the direction of world economic development and saw the possibility of and conditions for opening-up in China. Deng Xiaoping made the following statements in September 1978, when the issue of opening-up was proposed for the first time:

"Now we have many conditions for realizing the four modernizations (modernization of agriculture, industry, national defense and science and technology) which we didn't have when Mao Zedong was alive. If the Central Committee doesn't ponder problems and make up its mind based on existing conditions, it cannot propose and address many issues... After years of great efforts, today we have many more favorable international conditions so that we can absorb international advanced technologies, operational and management experience and capital. We didn't have such conditions when Mao Zedong was alive."[13] Indeed, the development trend of a new round of economic globalization occurred in the 1970s. Deng Xiaoping's opening-up policy grasped the rare opportunity of economic globalization to promote the overall development of China.

Noticeably, an anti-globalization trend appeared in the late 1990s, and kept growing when this round of economic globalization rapidly developed in the mid-1990s and became the most distinctive feature of world economic development. On November 30, 1999, when the Third WTO Ministerial Conference opened in Seattle, 40,000 globalization opponents gathered and protested, battling with policemen outside the venue. This protest marked the beginning of anti-globalization on a world scale. Now two international forums confront each other. One is the Davos-headquartered World Economic Forum, founded in 1971, which intensively voices economic globalization. The other is the World Social Forum, founded in Porto Alegre in Brazil in 2001, which intensively reflects anti-globalization demands. As a result, the CPC faces a challenge: to participate in economic globalization or participate in anti-globalization?

The Central Committee with Jiang Zemin at the core studied this issue. As emphasized by Jiang Zemin, "Economic globalization is the objective requirement and inevitable result of the development of the social productive forces. It facilitates optimized allocation of the means of production on a global scale and brings new development opportunities." "At the same time, we must be keenly aware that economic globalization is a double-edged sword," and "economic globalization not only intensifies competition in capital, technology, market and resources among developed countries, among developing countries and between developed countries and developing countries, it also aggravates contradictions between the rich and the poor in some countries and triggers off social conflicts." [14] Jiang Zemin made a strategic choice to participate in economic globalization while independently safeguarding China's economic security.

China has blazed a development path of independently building socialism with Chinese characteristics amidst integration into economic globalization from the opening-up proposed by Deng Xiaoping and participation in economic globalization decided by Jiang Zemin. By following this path China pursues mutual benefits in competition in the international market instead of raising our international standing by military expansion or group confrontation, and thus this path is also called the development path of peaceful rise. This path is another very important historical characteristic in the course of forming and developing socialism with Chinese characteristics.

The two historical characteristics suggest that, as emphasized by the CPC Central Committee on many occasions, we should grasp the development direction amidst the mutual connections of the domestic and international situations, make use of development opportunities amidst mutual translation of domestic and international conditions, create conditions for development amidst mutual supplementation of domestic and international resources, and control the overall development amidst the comprehensive utilization of domestic and international factors.

Formation of Cognition and Proposal of Topic

These vivid practices of reform and opening-up provide living experience for deepening the understanding of socialism. Since the Third Plenary Session of the 11th CPC Central Committee, the Party has always adhered to theoretical innovation and theoretical summarization to improve and develop our scientific understanding of socialism by summarizing practical experience. When summarizing the Party's historical experience, the Sixth Plenary Session of the 11th CPC Central Committee preliminarily summarized for the first time issues to be addressed by China such as social principal contradiction and center of work, steps and stages of modernization, reform and improvement of the socialist relations of production, correct handling of class struggle existing within a certain scope, and the promotion of socialist democracy as well as cultural and ethical progress.

Explicitly stated, these were the "cardinal points" of the "correct path of socialist modernization suited to China's reality" established by the Party since the Third Plenary Session of the 11th CPC Central Committee.[15]

In the process of profound rectification and creative exploration, Deng Xiaoping began to ponder the important basic issue of what kind of socialism China should build. The 12th CPC National Congress convened in September 1982 was the first Party congress after China entered the new stage of reform and opening-up and socialist modernization. At this important historical moment, Deng Xiaoping proposed the "basic conclusion" originating from practices of "taking our own path and building socialism with Chinese characteristics" in his opening speech at the Congress.[16]

Following the Third Plenary Session of the 11th CPC Central Committee, the Party's second generation of central collective leadership with Deng Xiaoping at the core made the most far-reaching and significant transformation in the Party's history since the founding of New China in leading all Party members and Chinese people to bring order out of chaos and implement reform in an all-round way, put forward the scientific topic of "taking the path of socialism with Chinese characteristics" and blazed a unique development path for socialism.

Severe Test at a Historical Juncture

Jiang Zemin frequently described the arduous efforts we made to build socialism with Chinese characteristics by "You never know what you can do till you try." Before the Third Plenary Session of the 11th CPC Central Committee, we had made arduous efforts to explore a way for Chinese socialist construction; we took an uneven path after the session. Differently, the arduous efforts before the session were mainly embodied by tortuous exploration, for which the Party and Chinese people paid a heavy cost, while the arduous efforts after the session were mainly demonstrated by stiff and complicated pioneering and innovation during which the Party and Chinese people went through severe tests one after another.

Looking back at the explorations of reform and opening-up, we can see that China stood tests at five crucial historical junctures.

The first test came after the "cultural revolution." Should China continue to adhere to the theory of "continuous revolution under the condition of dictatorship of the proletariat" and the basic line of "taking class struggle as the key link" based on the "Two Whatevers" or should it deny the Four Cardinal Principles and engage in bourgeois liberalization? At this critical moment, Deng Xiaoping resolutely and boldly negated these two wrong views, published the *Emancipate the Mind, Seek Truth from Facts and Unite to Face the Future*, a declaration initiating the new theory of Chinese Marxism, in 1978, and re-established the ideological line of "emancipating the mind and seeking truth from facts," thus laying a foundation for developing the basic line of taking economic development as the central task and blazing a new path of socialist construction in the new period. After making the statement that we should "take our own path of building socialism with Chinese characteristics" at the 12th CPC National Congress, senior Party members represented by Deng Xiaoping further summarized China's historical experience in socialist construction and new experience in reform and opening-up in particular, drew the lessons from the Soviet model and its effects on China, and profoundly explored the path of socialism with Chinese characteristics. The Third Plenary Session of the 12th CPC Central Committee, in particular, broke away from the traditional concept of opposing the planned economy to the commodity economy and put forward the idea of developing a socialist commodity economy. Meanwhile, Deng Xiaoping repeatedly emphasized that we must take a firm position against bourgeois liberalization when he led the reform and opening-up. The 13th CPC National Congress systematically expounded the theory of the primary stage of socialism and developed the Party's basic line of "One Central Task and Two Basic Points" in this stage, i.e. taking economic development as the central task and adhering to the Four Cardinal Principles and the policy of reform and opening-up.

The second test occurred at the critical historical juncture when China faced the severe test of domestic and international political turmoil in the late 1980s and early 1990s. Should China let bourgeois liberalization run rampant and let the collapse of the former Soviet Union and tremendous changes in Eastern Europe push down the Great Wall of Chinese socialism or regard reform and opening-up as the introduction and development of capitalism and regard reform in the economic field as the primary hazard of peaceful evolution? At the critical moment, Deng Xiaoping suppressed interference from both the right and left wingers, and in 1992 published his famous *Talks in the South* — a declaration that drove reform and opening-up and modernization to a new stage, emphasized that we must firmly adhere to the basic line for 100 years and that development is the absolute principle. He answered questions about the socialist or capitalist market economy, pointing out a direction for exploring a new path of emancipating and developing the productive forces under the conditions of a socialist market economy.

The Party's central collective leadership then with Jiang Zemin at the core profoundly summarized China's lessons and experience since the introduction of the policies of socialist construction and reform and opening-up on the one hand, and profoundly reflected on the lessons and experience of socialist movements all over the world and in particular the collapse of the former Soviet Union and tremendous changes in Eastern Europe, and continued to deepen its understanding of the path of socialism with Chinese characteristics. Noticeably, the 14th CPC National Congress proposed that the whole Party should be equipped with Deng Xiaoping's theory of building socialism with Chinese characteristics, determined the reform goal of building a socialist market economic system, and raised the point of speeding up the efforts to promote material progress while focusing on promoting ethical and cultural progress, the Party's building and political progress so as to correct the mistake of "attaching importance to material progress while neglecting ethical and cultural progress." We further improved and developed our understanding of the path of socialism with Chinese characteristics in the course of promoting the development of the socialist cause with Chinese characteristics in an all-round way.

The third test was that China was at the crucial historical juncture of choice of direction after Deng Xiaoping passed away. As the economic system reform had entered a critical stage and development was in complicated critical period, should China retake the old path of unitary public ownership and planned economy or seek a way out via "privatization"? At that critical moment, the Party's third generation of central collective leadership with Jiang Zemin at the core resolutely withstood pressure from left and right, and made a historical decision at the 15th CPC National Congress to write Deng Xiaoping Theory into the Party's Constitution as part of the Party's guiding thought. Meanwhile, the Party developed its basic program of the primary stage of socialism, clearly established the basic economic system in which public ownership is the mainstay and economic entities of diverse ownership develop together in the primary stage of socialism, emphasized that we must comprehensively understand public ownership and allow diversified forms of realizing public ownership instead of generally defining the shareholding system as "capitalist" or "socialist," and made strategic decisions to get involved in economic globalization and accede to the WTO in an all-round way, thus comprehensively driving the building of socialism with Chinese characteristics to the 21st century in a new round of emancipating the mind.

The fourth test was that the Party was at a crucial historical juncture at the turn of the century regarding how to grasp the strategic opportunity to most extensively mobilize all positive factors to build a moderately prosperous society in all respects. Should China doggedly ignore changes in the Party's historical position as well as profound changes in social life and social structure during the reform and opening-up or change the Party's nature and purpose and give up principle because of changes in the Party and society? At that critical moment, the Party's third generation of central collective leadership with Jiang Zemin at the core responded to challenges from various wrong views, proposed the important thought of the Three Represents, published the important speech by Jiang Zemin at the celebration of the 80th Anniversary of the Communist Party of China, and in particular decided at the 16th CPC National Congress to write the important thought of the Three Represents into the Party's Constitution as a long-term guiding thought that the Party must adhere to. Meanwhile, the Party explicitly defined the new social classes appearing in the course of the reform and opening-up as the builders of socialism with Chinese characteristics on the one hand, and stressed that we must care for the production and living of people in straitened circumstances, and seriously consider the interests of people of different classes on the other hand, so as to comprehensively implement the Party's fundamental principle, constantly strengthen its class basis, expand its mass basis, and finish the historical task of building a moderately prosperous society in all respects.

The fifth test was that the Party faced numerous domestic and foreign risks as well as risks from nature, the economy and society in the new century. China's economic and social development showed new-stage characteristics when China had accomplished significant achievements in socialism with

Chinese characteristics. In the face of the coexisting golden period for development and period of sharp contradictions as well as difficulties and problems in practice, should China stick to the old measures practiced before the reform and opening-up or copy Western measures to address problems? China faced a choice of direction and path in the critical period of developing socialism with Chinese characteristics. The Party members represented by Hu Jintao took a clear-cut stand: We will hold high the great banner of socialism with Chinese characteristics, regarding Deng Xiaoping Theory and the important thought of the Three Represents as guiding principles, thoroughly apply the Scientific Outlook on Development, continue to emancipate the mind, adhere to reform and opening-up, push forward scientific development, promote social harmony and strive to win a new victory in building a moderately prosperous society in all aspects.

Since the 16th CPC National Congress, the Party's central collective leadership with Hu Jintao as General Secretary, guided by Deng Xiaoping Theory and the important thought of the Three Represents, further deepened the understanding of the path of socialism with Chinese characteristics by profoundly analyzing the characteristics of economic and social development in the new century, conscientiously summarizing experience and existing problems in development and referring to the development experience of foreign countries. In particular, the Third Plenary Session of the 16th CPC Central Committee proposed that we seek people-oriented, comprehensive, balanced and sustainable development, and the Fourth Plenary Session of the 16th CPC Central Committee stated we would build a harmonious socialist society and included the task in the overall layout of socialism with Chinese characteristics together with the development of a socialist market economy, socialist democracy and socialist advanced culture. On this basis, the 17th CPC National Congress profoundly expounded the relationship between the path and the banner of socialism with Chinese characteristics as well as the relationship between the path and the system of theories of socialism with Chinese characteristics, profoundly elaborated the essential characteristics and scientific connotations of the path of socialism with Chinese characteristics for the first time, and answered significant strategic questions that concern China's long-term development of what is the path of socialism with Chinese characteristics and how to adhere to this path.

Hu Jintao said, "The Party has opened the path of socialism with Chinese characteristics in the new period because we have theoretically and scientifically inherited Marxism-Leninism and Mao Zedong Thought, correctly grasped the international situations and characteristics of the times, comprehensively summarized both positive and negative experiences in domestic and foreign socialism building, and profoundly understood the practices of China's reform and opening-up and socialist modernization as well as the common aspirations of all the people." [17]

Historical Dialectics

Looking back on the five challenges to the Party and the Chinese people in the course of exploring the path of socialism with Chinese characteristics, we clearly see that our explorations are constantly expanded and deepened by following economic laws. The logic of the course of the past over 30 years is very clear:

1   In order to address the principal social contradictions in contemporary China, we should take economic development as the central task, adhere to the Four Cardinal Principles and the policy of reform and opening-up, and continue to release and develop the productive forces, which was an issue proposed and addressed by the Party at the first critical historical juncture;

2   In order to release and develop the productive forces, we should deepen reform and opening-up, and develop a socialist market economy, which was a topic proposed and explored by the Party at the second critical historical juncture;

3   In order to build a socialist market economy system, we should establish a basic economic system in which public

ownership is the mainstay and economic entities of diverse ownership develop together, and adopt diversified forms such as the shareholding system to realize public ownership so as to meet the needs of a socialized, market-based and modern economy, which was a challenge overcome by the Party at the third crucial historical juncture;

4　In order to develop the basic economic system in which public ownership is the mainstay and economic entities of diverse ownership develop together and build a socialist market economy based on such a basic economic system, we should correctly understand and handle the new social classes appearing in the course of reform and opening-up, take the interests of all classes and people into account, and integrate such classes and people into the basis for the Party's governance to jointly finish the historical tasks of socialist modernization and the great rejuvenation of the Chinese nation, which was a complicated issue put forward and handled by the Party at the fourth crucial historical juncture;

5　In order to give full play to all forces, we should put forward the Scientific Outlook on Development characterized by people orientation and comprehensive, balanced and sustainable development, accelerate the improvement in the change of the growth mode and combine balanced development with social harmony, which was an issue proposed and handled by the Party at the fifth critical historical juncture. We have advanced in a pioneering spirit in the course of gradually and profoundly understanding and addressing difficulties in development.

Looking back at the five tests at critical historical junctures for the Party and the Chinese people in the course of exploring the path of socialism with Chinese characteristics, we also clearly see the arduous tasks of leading and advancing the new revolution of reform and opening-up as well as the inherent logic of the measures we have taken. This logic requires us to keep abreast of the times in addressing contradictions one after another in life instead of reasoning dogmatically. This means that we should pursue the "objective dialectics" defined by the founders of Marxism as well as the "historical dialectics" defined by Mao Zedong.

The Chinese Path is a path that meets China's reality and the dialectics of Chinese history, and contributes to the country's prosperity and the people's well-being. Simply put, it is a path meeting the Tao.

Two Unavoidable Questions

Mao Zedong's Exploration of Socialism in China

Ideological Wealth Left by Mao Zedong

Mao Zedong and Deng Xiaoping: Relationship Between Explorations Before and After the Reform and Opening-up Era

In the course of exploring the path of socialism with Chinese characteristics, people frequently talk about the relationship between Mao Zedong and Deng Xiaoping, with some people saying that there were contradictions between Mao and Deng. The Party pays special attention to and is soberly aware of and prudent about this issue, to which Deng Xiaoping, Jiang Zemin, Hu Jintao and Xi Jinping took a consistently distinct attitude and gave scientific discourses full of dialectical philosophy.

Two Unavoidable Questions

We can't avoid two questions when researching and discussing the formation and development history of the path of socialism with Chinese characteristics: Did Mao Zedong make a contribution to blazing the trail of socialism with Chinese characteristics and what is the relationship between the two historical periods before and after the introduction of the reform and opening-up policies?

The Party answered the first question at the 18th CPC National Congress. *The Report to the 18th CPC National Congress* comprehensively expounded the question by noting "four successes" in the two historical periods. Mao Zedong "successfully accomplished the most profound and the greatest social transformation in China's history" and "provided invaluable experience as well as a theoretical and material basis for launching the great initiative of building socialism with Chinese characteristics in the new historical period"; Deng Xiaoping "successfully launched the great initiative of building socialism with Chinese characteristics," Jiang Zemin "successfully advanced socialism with Chinese characteristics into the 21st century" and Hu Jintao successfully "upheld and developed socialism with Chinese characteristics from a new historical starting point."[18] The *Report* elaborated on the contributions made by Mao Zedong to the building of socialism with Chinese characteristics and stated that Deng Xiaoping was the pioneer of socialism with Chinese characteristics. In other words, the two historical periods are divided by the creation of socialism with Chinese characteristics. We must acknowledge the contributions made by Mao Zedong in paving the way and clearly understand that socialism with Chinese characteristics was launched by Deng Xiaoping at the Third Plenary Session of the 11th CPC Central Committee.

Some people may ask: Since Mao Zedong provided invaluable experience as well as a theoretical and material basis for launching the great initiative of building socialism with Chinese characteristics in the new historical period, why was socialism with Chinese characteristics not pioneered by Mao Zedong? Mao

Zedong "suffered serious setbacks" in the course of socialist development and in particular put forward and insisted on, till he passed away, the theory of "continuous revolution under the dictatorship of the proletariat" that entirely went against the guiding ideology in the early stage of his exploration. We inherited valuable ideological wealth from Mao Zedong after clarifying confusion and bringing things back to order. While we can't deny Mao Zedong's contributions to today's socialism with Chinese characteristics just because of the serious mistakes he made in his later years, we must be soberly aware that what Mao Zedong adhered to in his later years was not socialism with Chinese characteristics. Socialism with Chinese characteristics is a brand-new cause based on clearing up confusion, and reform and opening-up, so our discussion on this question can't depart from the reality of the historical process.

General Secretary Xi Jinping also elaborated on the second question: "The building of socialism under the Party's leadership is divided into two historical periods — before and after the introduction of the reform and opening-up policies, which are related yet differ greatly from each other." This was pointed out by Xi Jinping on January 5, 2013 at the Seminar on Learning and Applying the Spirit of the 18th CPC National Congress by New Members and Alternate Members of the Central Committee held by the Central Party School. The two periods differ greatly from each other because "there are great differences in reform and opening-up, in the guiding ideology, guideline, policy and actual work of socialist construction, and in that socialism with Chinese characteristics was pioneered in the new historical period of reform and opening-up." They are interrelated because the two historical periods "are essentially practical explorations in the building of socialism by the people under the Party's leadership"; socialism with Chinese characteristics was initiated when New China had already established a basic socialist system and had been building socialism for more than 20 years." Therefore, Xi Jinping said the two historical periods "are by no means separated and fundamentally opposite, so we can't negate the historical period before reform and opening-up by the one after the reform and opening-up, and vice versa."[19]

Mao Zedong's Exploration of Socialism in China

In order to answer these two questions about which people are very concerned, we will simply review the arduous exploration of Chinese socialist construction by Mao Zedong before the introduction of the reform and opening-up policies:

In 1956 China completed the transition from new democracy

to socialism, and entered socialist society in the course of the socialist transformation of the means of production. Since China went through so many setbacks in the period of democratic revolution, Mao Zedong once hoped that we could make fewer detours to build socialism. However, practice told us we still needed to make creative and arduous efforts to explore the building of socialism, which was an unprecedented brand-new cause in this economically and culturally backward country.

Against such a backdrop, Mao Zedong put forward the important thought of "second application of Marxism." He said, "In the period of socialist revolution and construction, we must make a second application of Marxism to find the correct path for socialist revolution and construction in China." Mao pointed this out in April 1956, when he discussed the Soviet Union's historical experience in building socialism. [20]

The "second application of Marxism" is relative to the "application" in the period of the democratic revolution. The Party found the correct path for the Chinese revolution and won a great victory in the new democratic revolution by applying the universal truths of Marxism to the specific practices of the Chinese revolution for the first time. However, one "application" is not efficacious forever and we need to make a new "application" in the face of new practices and historical tasks. The "second application of Marxism" put forward by Mao Zedong indicates that the Party already realized the arduous historical task of the building of Chinese socialism at that time.

The focus of the "second application of Marxism" was to find a path of socialist construction based on China's realities. Mao Zedong always believed that we should independently explore revolution and construction instead of copying the experience of foreign countries. However, we had no choice but to learn from the experience of the Soviet Union – the first socialist country – as we had no experience of economic development in the early stage after the founding of New China in 1949. As a result, our systems, mechanisms and policies reflected those of the Soviet Union in many respects. In the mid-1950s we found that some experiences of the Soviet Union were not entirely suitable for China's national conditions. Against such a backdrop, Mao Zedong proposed, after prudent consideration, that we should "take the Soviet Union as a mirror" and independently explore a path of Chinese socialist construction that was different from the Soviet Model but was suitable for China's national conditions.

Mao Zedong published *On the Ten Major Relationships* on April 25, 1956, in which he pointed out, "In particular, recently the Soviet Union has exposed some disadvantages and mistakes in the course of socialist construction. Do you want to take the roundabout courses they took? In the past, we made fewer detours by referring to their experience and lessons. Now of course we must regard the Soviet Union as a mirror."[21] This statement marked the beginning of the exploration of the path of socialist construction suitable for China's national conditions by the Party's first generation of collective leadership. From then on, his exploration was divided into two stages by the launch of the "cultural revolution" in May 1966 – namely 10 years before the "cultural revolution," during which China built socialism in an all-round way, and 10 years of the "cultural revolution" during which the Party and country suffered serious setbacks in socialist practice.

The first stage lasted for 10 years, starting from China's basic completion of the socialist transformation of private ownership of the means of production and transition to comprehensive large-scale socialist construction by the people of all ethnic groups under the Party's leadership in 1956 to the launch of the "cultural revolution" in 1966.

In this stage, the Party made serious mistakes in guidelines and underwent a tortuous course of development mainly evidenced by four fluctuations:

The first fluctuation took place in the period 1956-1957. After the Eighth CPC National Congress in 1956 all the people devoted themselves to a vigorous upsurge of socialist construction under the Party's leadership. The Party decided to launch the Rectification Movement to better arouse the people's enthusiasm for socialism and correct the subjectivism, bureaucratism and

sectarianism that occurred in the Party's work. A handful of "right
wingers" publicly challenged the Party's authoritative leadership
when the people supported the rectification under the Party's
leadership, and thus the rectification movement immediately
changed into an anti-rightist struggle. Unexpectedly, the Party
made the mistake of expanding the anti-rightist struggle in 1957,
hampering the enthusiasm of the people and intellectuals in
particular for socialism.

The second fluctuation occurred in the period 1957-
1958. After the anti-rightist struggle, the Party proposed the
shift of work focus to the new task of technological revolution
after winning a victory in socialist revolution at the political
ideological frontline based on the principle of integrating the
theory of uninterrupted revolution with the theory of the
development of revolution by stages. The Second Session of the
Eighth CPC National Congress developed the general line of "go
ahead with all efforts and build socialism with more outcome,
higher speed, better quality and less cost," and the Chinese
people pushed ahead with socialist construction under the
Party's leadership. However, the Party too vigorously stressed
subjective enthusiasm and ignored the objective law of economic
development. Consequently, the Party made the mistakes of
the "Great Leap Forward" and the Campaign for the People's
Communes in rural areas, and so socialist construction suffered

another serious setback.

The third fluctuation occurred in the period 1958-1959. At the end of 1958 Mao Zedong found problems in the Great Leap Forward and the Campaign for the People's Communes, and strove to correct the mistakes. However, unexpectedly, a campaign against Right deviation sprang up again in the later stage of an important conference held at Mt. Lushan in 1959, thus interrupting the process of intra-Party democracy and the process of correcting Left deviations in economic policies.

The fourth fluctuation occurred in the period 1959-1966. Due to errors in guidance, serious natural disasters and breaches of contract by the Soviet Union, China's national economy was in serious difficulties, as a result of which the country and people suffered heavy losses. In the winter of 1960 the CPC Central Committee and Mao Zedong began to correct the mistake of Left deviation in rural work, formed a series of important thoughts on socialist construction, including the development of socialist commodity production, decided to "adjust, consolidate, enrich and improve" the national economy, worked out important documents that promoted the positive and sound development of socialist agriculture, industry and education, removed the label from most "rightists" and rehabilitated most people who had been wrongly criticized during the movement against Right deviations. As a result, China's national economy was revitalized in the period 1962-1966. However, the erroneous work style of officials, poor economic management and other problems cropped up in the course of national economic recovery and development, and Mao Zedong became soberly aware of these problems. At the Tenth Plenary Session of the Eighth CPC Central Committee in 1962 he put forward the issue of class struggle again, asserting that the bourgeoisie would continue to exist and attempt comeback in the whole historical stage of socialism which would became the source of intra-Party revisionism. In 1963 Mao made the call to "take class struggle as the key link," launched the socialist education movement in some rural areas and a few cities in the period 1963-1965, and stated that the movement's focus was to punish the so-called "senior Party officials taking the capitalist road." In that period, many cultural and artistic works, academic viewpoints and some representative figures in cultural, artistic and academic circles were wrongly and excessively criticized from a political standpoint.

At the same time, the Party gained important experience in leading socialist construction. China's national industrial fixed assets had grown by three times by 1966 compared with 1956. The output of major industrial products such as cotton yarn, raw coal, power-generating capacity, crude oil, steel and mechanical equipment had grown considerably. China realized independence in oil in 1965, set up a group of emerging industrial sectors such as the electronics industry and petrochemicals industry, and improved the layout of industrial development. Moreover, China began to launch basic construction and technological transformation of agriculture on a large scale. The consumption of agricultural tractors and chemical fertilizers increased by over six times, and rural power consumption grew by 70 times. The number of graduates from institutions of higher learning increased by 4.9 times compared with seven years previously. The quality of education was significantly improved after some rectification, and outstanding achievements were accomplished in science and technology. The material and technological base on which we now depend for modernization was mainly built in that period, and most experts in economic and cultural development were trained in that period. In particular, at the Third National People's Congress, convened in late 1964 and early 1965, Premier Zhou Enlai, as proposed by Mao Zedong, announced that we would strive to turn China into a socialist power with modern agriculture, industry, national defense and science and technology. Inspired by this ambitious goal, the people of all ethnic groups worked hard and made great achievements relying on their own efforts. This was the dominant element in the Party's work in this period.

The second stage also lasted for 10 years — from the "cultural revolution" launched in 1966 to the downfall of the

"Gang of Four" in 1976. It is necessary for us to define clearly
the movement and the period of the "cultural revolution." The
first was civil strife that was launched by the Party leader by
mistake and was taken advantage of by the anti-revolution
gang, and brought a series of disasters to the Party, the country
and the people of all ethnic groups. The period of the "cultural
revolution" was the historical period from 1966 to 1976. In this
historical period the Party and the people kept fighting against
"left" adventurism as well as the Lin Biao and Jiang Qing anti-
revolution gangs. The concerted struggle of the whole Party,
workers, farmers, officers and soldiers of the People's Liberation
Army, intellectuals, educated youths and officials limited the
damage of the momentum of the "cultural revolution" to a certain
extent. In particular, the Party and people eventually defeated
the Lin Biao and Jiang Qing anti-revolution gangs. The nature of
the Communist Party of China, the people's regime, the people's
army and the whole of society were not changed. History proved
once again that the Chinese people and the Party are great, and
China's socialist system has a great and strong vitality.

In short, in the two decades of arduous exploration from
1956 to 1976 we accomplished great historical achievements and
made big mistakes due to complicated subjective and objective
reasons including complicated domestic and international
situations. Great historical achievements mainly included the

proposal of many valuable views and opinions, preliminary opening of the path of Chinese socialist construction in practice, establishment of an independent and complete industrial system and national economic system, and significant progress in socialist industrialization. The big mistakes mainly included the mistakes of the Great Leap Forward and the Campaign for the People's Communes, and in particular the decade-long civil strife of the "cultural revolution." Regrettably, in the face of these big mistakes in practice, theoretical work went wrong. We proposed the theory of "continuous revolution under the dictatorship of the proletariat" and developed the basic line of "taking class struggle as the key link." These ideological and theoretical mistakes not only changed the direction and requirement of the "second application of Marxism" put forward by the Party in the early stage of socialist construction, they also devastated Chinese socialism. However, both great historical achievements and big mistakes are valuable wealth accumulated by the Party in the course of building a base for socialism in China's national conditions and constituted an important basis for the Party to lead all the people to open the path of socialism with Chinese characteristics in the period following the introduction of the reform and opening-up policies.

Ideological Wealth Left by Mao Zedong

To expound on the ideological wealth left by Mao Zedong,
let's first learn about the valuable views and proposals left by the
Party's first generation of collective leadership with Comrade Mao
Zedong at the core:

1   Long-term socialism and stages of development. "China
has just established and has not completely improved and
consolidated the socialist system,"[22] said Mao Zedong in the
early years after China entered socialist society. At that time, Mao
Zedong put forward the view that the building of socialism is long-
term and arduous. After the setbacks of the Great Leap Forward
and the Campaign for the People's Communes, Mao Zedong further
proposed the issue of stages of socialist development. In the
history of the development of scientific socialism, Marx stated,
from the perspective of development in terms of materialistic
dialectics, that socialist society in the future will go from the "first
stage" to "developed stage," but failed to discuss whether every
development stage is divided into sub-stages. Lenin stated that
in socialist practice every development stage has a multilevel
development process, i.e. each big stage is composed of small
stages. As influenced by the Soviet model, nearly all socialist
countries used to regard socialist society as a short stage and were
anxious to make the transition to communism. By summarizing

lessons and experience in this regard, Mao Zedong came up with the important judgment that socialism is a very long historical stage. As pointed out by Mao in late 1959, when he read the Soviet textbook, *Plutonomy for Socialism* that socialism can be divided into two stages, namely underdeveloped socialism in which China was and developed socialism which may take a longer time than the former. This was a profound understanding of China's national conditions and stage of socialist development.

2   Theory of social contradictions of socialism. Mao Zedong was a great Marxist theorist who always paid attention to creating new theories and writing new works based on practice and guiding new practices and addressing new issues by innovative theories. The greatest theory created by Mao Zedong in the socialist period was that of the social contradictions of socialism, which was an important theoretical foundation for the path of Chinese socialist construction. Marx and Engels founded historical materialism, and believed that all societies moved forward driven by the basic social contradictions of the productive forces and productive relations as well as the economic base and superstructure. They did not discuss what the driving force for the development of society in the future would be which would replace capitalism. "Confrontation and contradiction are totally different. In socialist society, confrontation will disappear but contradiction will still exist,"[23] said Lenin when he annotated and commented on *Economics in*

the *Transition Period* by Bukharin in 1920. Stalin analyzed the social contradictions in the Soviet Union in the early 1930s by using "internal contradiction" (contradiction between workers and the peasants) and "external contradiction" (contradiction between the Soviet Union and the capitalist countries). However, after announcing that the Soviet Union had entered the stage of socialist society in 1936, Stalin said that he believed the productive forces and productive relations in the socialist society of the Soviet Union "entirely suited" each other, and emphasized moral and political consistency as the driving force behind the development of Soviet society. As influenced by Stalin, the metaphysical view of "the theory that no contradictions exist in socialist society" dominated the Soviet Union's academic circles for a long time. Stalin later discovered contradictions in real society, but thought that they were caused by policy problems, without realizing that contradictions existed objectively in socialist society.

Therefore, in his *On the Correct Handling of Contradictions among the People*, Mao Zedong comprehensively applied the views stated in his famous work *On Contradiction* to socialist society and emphasized that contradictions exist in all aspects of socialist society, and that contradictions are the fundamental driving force behind the development of socialist society. Mao was the first person to incisively analyze the contradictions of socialist society in the history of socialist ideology. He focused on analyzing two kinds of contradictions. The first was the basic contradiction of socialist society — between productive relations and productive forces as well as between superstructure and economic base. Different from contradictions in the old society, the two sides of the contradictions match and conflict with each other. Mao Zedong's statement represents a big step forward compared with Stalin's "entirely suited" theory, greatly emancipated the Chinese people's minds, and provided a most important theoretical basis for later reform. The second one was social contradictions of different natures in socialist society. Aimed at Soviet Union's expansion of the campaign against counterrevolutionaries, Mao Zedong stated that there are contradictions of different natures — those among the people and those between us and the enemy — in socialist society. He stressed that we should strictly distinguish and correctly handle these two kinds of contradictions as they have different natures. After the large-scale violent class struggle in the revolutionary period has basically ended, a large number of contradictions are those among the people, so we should regard the correct handling of contradictions among the people as the major work of the country's political life. This provided an important theoretical demonstration for mobilizing all positive factors to build socialism.

3   Chinese path of industrialization. To realize development, China must accomplish socialist industrialization and turn itself from a backward agricultural country into an advanced

industrial country. In consideration of a wide range of problems existing in industrialization in the Soviet Union, Mao Zedong stated that we must take a Chinese path of industrialization different from that of the Soviet model. Based on China's national conditions, to realize China's industrialization, we should first arrange the national economy by following the order of agriculture, light industry and heavy industry, adjust the industrial structure and investment proportion and regard such adjustment as the overall guideline of economic construction. Second, we should promote the common development of industry in coastal and inland areas, place more emphasis on leveraging and developing coastal industry and vigorously develop inland industry to balance the layout of industrial development. Third, we should build national defense based on economic development. Mao Zedong pointed out that we should strengthen national defense building, and manufacture airplanes, cannons and an atomic bomb. However, national defense building should be based on economic development. Only rapid economic development could help us make greater progress in national defense building.

4   Goals and steps of Chinese socialist modernization. Realizing industrialization to turn China into an advanced industrial country from a backward agricultural country was only the first step, and the higher goal was to realize socialist modernization. The CPC Central Committee put forward the goal of socialist mod-

ernization as early as in 1954. In 1964 the then Premier Zhou Enlai further stated in the *Report on the Work of the Government* delivered at the First Session of the Third National People's Congress that China would comprehensively realize the four modernizations of agriculture, industry, national defense, and science and technology. To this end, China would adopt a two-step development strategy. For the first step, China would spend 15 years up until 1980 to build an independent and complete industrial system and national economic system; for the second step, China would complete the four modernizations by 2000 to turn itself into one of the world's leading economic powers.

5   Reforming the Party's leadership system and socialist economic system, and mobilizing all positive factors to build socialism. By regarding the thought of the correct handling of contradictions among the people as the theoretical basis, Mao Zedong believed that to build socialism we must mobilize all positive factors, translate negative factors into positive ones and unite with all forces that can be united with. He clearly pointed out that this was the basic guideline for China to build socialism. Based on this guideline, Mao required us to correctly handle a series of important relations in socialist construction, and reform the Party's leadership system and socialist economic system. First, the relationship between the central and local governments. While consolidating the unified leadership of the

central government, we should delegate more powers to local governments so as to give full play to the enthusiasm of both the central and local governments. Second, the relationship between the CPC and the non-communist parties. Mao argued that several coexisting parties are better than only one, and that we must adhere to "long-term coexistence and mutual supervision" for the CPC and the other parties. Third, the relationship among the country, collective and individual. We must give full consideration to the country, collective and individual (take into consideration both the army and the people as well as both public and private interests) instead of only taking into consideration the country and the collective. Fourth, the relationship between the Han people and the ethnic minorities. The Han must sincerely and actively help the ethnic minorities to develop their economies and cultures. Fifth, the relationship between China and foreign countries. China must learn favorable factors from foreign countries with analysis and discretion instead of blindly imitating and mechanically copying their experiences. Of course we should not copy their blemishes and shortcomings.[24] The correct handling of these relationships is of great significance. Mao pointed out that "we must strive to mobilize all positive factors, direct and indirect, within and outside the Party, and both at home and abroad, to turn China into a powerful socialist country."[25]

    6   Developing socialist commodity production and com-

modity exchange. Targeting the wrong tendency of fear and objection to the commodity production of the Soviet Union, and some Chinese economists, Mao Zedong severely criticized these "poor Marxists." He broke away from the thought of the founder of Marxism and agreed with the views stated by Stalin in the latter's *Socialist Economic Issues in the Soviet Union*, believing that commodity production also exists in socialist society, and requiring us to vigorously develop commodity production and commodity exchange. He also pointed out that the law of value is a great school which can teach millions of officials and tens of millions of people to build socialism and communism.

7   Socialist democratic political construction. Mao Zedong emphasized that we must expand socialist democracy and oppose bureaucratism, vigorously develop socialist legal construction and ensure "there are laws to abide by and that all laws are strictly observed," prevent bureaucratic practices and the emergence of cliques and prevent officials and leaders at all levels from becoming a special class, adhere to democratic centralism and create a "lively political situation characterized by the coexistence of centralism and democracy, discipline and freedom, as well as unified will and individual feeling."[26]

8   Implementing the policy of having "a hundred flowers bloom and a hundred schools of thought contend" in the cultural field. Socialist construction includes both economic construction

and cultural construction. The Soviet Union controlled culture too tightly, frequently used administrative means for academic management and politically labeled different schools. For example, the Michurin School was supposed to be materialistic while the Morgan School was called idealistic. The Soviet Union regarded the Michurin School as an academic authority and suppressed the Morgan School, which inevitably stifled the development of science. Targeting this situation, Mao stated that China must implement the policy of having "a hundred flowers bloom and a hundred schools of thought contend" in the cultural field to promote artistic development and scientific progress as well as the prosperity of socialist culture in China. Implementing one style and one school while prohibiting others by administrative means only harms the development of art and science. To implement the policy, we must, guided by Marxism, well handle the relationship between a hundred schools and one school of thought; otherwise we will lose the correct political direction.

9　Implementing an independent foreign policy of peace. After the founding of New China in 1949, Mao Zedong and Zhou Enlai developed an independent foreign policy of peace that was not controlled by capitalism or one socialist power. Based on the thoughts of two systems and peaceful coexistence of Lenin, Zhou Enlai further proposed the Five Principles of Peaceful

Coexistence as the criteria for mutual relations among countries with different social systems, fostering a favorable international environment for China's modernization. In the early 1970s, Mao Zedong presented the theory of the "Three Worlds," based on the world situation to form an extensive international united front and expand China's foreign contacts.

10 Strengthening Party's building. The Party is always the firm leadership core guiding the cause of socialism with Chinese characteristics. It is necessary to strengthen Party building to adhere to the Party's leadership. As pointed out by Mao Zedong, the Party faced a severe test of governance and should strengthen its building in ideology and theory, work style, opposition to bureaucracy, close contact with the people and resolute combat against corruption. In particular, Mao systematically expounded the principle of democratic centralism and proposed many important thoughts for better giving play to intra-Party democracy in the process of socialist construction in his *Speech at the Extended Central Work Conference* in 1962.

The above-mentioned aspects were scientific achievements and valuable ideological heritages left by Mao Zedong when exploring the path of Chinese socialist construction. This path differed from the Soviet Model, with a great breakthrough in the path of socialist industrialization, but still adhered to construction within the framework of a highly centralized planned economic system due to cognitive limitations of the people at that time. However, many good thoughts were not applied and implemented because Mao later changed his ideological understanding, overstated class struggle both at home and abroad, persisted in class struggle as the key link, deviated from the central task of economic development and even put forward many wrong theories such as "continuous revolution under the dictatorship of the proletariat." In particular, the "cultural revolution" nearly discontinued the exploration of the path. The positive achievements accomplished by the explorers of the path of the construction of socialism provide important ideological materials, theoretical preparations and preconditions for later generations to blaze the new trail of socialism with Chinese characteristics and establish a new socialist theory system with Chinese characteristics.

Some countries may not be happy with our matter-of-fact research and evaluation of Mao Zedong's contributions to and mistakes made in the exploration of socialism. However, as serious scholars, we can't accuse Mao Zedong or Deng Xiaoping flying in the face of the facts, nor should we artificially set up "contradictions" between Mao Zedong and Deng Xiaoping. As a matter of fact, Mao Zedong's explorations, experience and lessons in this field lay a hard-won foundation for explorations by later generations and reduce ideological barriers in the face of some complicated issues.

Cognitive Process of Scientific Connotation of the Chinese Path

Basic Elements of the Chinese Path

Not a Capitalist Path with Chinese Characteristics

Chinese Path:
Scientific Connotation and
Non-capitalist Nature

Some people may ask, "What is the 'Chinese Path' you are talking about?" I should have answered this question at the very beginning, but I bring it up here because the Party keeps deepening its understanding of the scientific connotations of the path of socialism with Chinese characteristics in practice.

Cognitive Process of Scientific Connotation of the Chinese Path

Although the exact concept of the "path of socialism with Chinese characteristics" had not taken shape in the resolutions on historical issues passed at the Sixth Plenary Session of the 11th CPC Central Committee, the resolutions summarized the "cardinal points" of "correct path of socialist construction that is suitable for China's national conditions." (1) The principal problem in our society to be addressed after the basic completion of socialist transformation is how we can meet the ever-growing material and cultural needs of the people with backward social production. The Party and country should shift the focus of work to socialist modernization with economic development as the central task, vigorously develop the social productive forces and gradually improve the people's material and cultural lives. (2) For socialist economic development, we must do what we are capable of based on China's national condition and realize the goal of modernization by steps and stages. (3) The reform and improvement of socialist relations of production must suit the condition of the productive forces and contribute to the development of production. (4) Class struggle is no longer the principle problem after the exploiting class is eliminated. Class struggle will exist for a long term to a certain degree and may be intensified under some conditions due to domestic factors and international influences. (5) Gradually building a highly democratic socialist political system is one of fundamental tasks of the socialist revolution. (6) Socialism must include high cultural and ethical progress. (7) Improving and developing socialist ethnic relations and strengthening ethnic solidarity are of important significance for China as a multi-ethnic country. (8) Under the international conditions of existing danger of war, we should strengthen modern national defense, the building of which must suit our economic development. (9) With regard to foreign relations, we must continue to fight against imperialism, hegemonism, colonialism and racialism, and safeguard world peace. (10) In consideration of the lessons of the "cultural revolution" and the Party's current situation, we must turn the Party into one equipped with complete democratic centralism.[27] These points represent the preliminary summarization of the development path of Chinese socialism before the proposal of "taking our own path and building socialism with Chinese characteristics" raised at the 12th CPC National Congress.

The scientific concept of the "path of socialism with Chinese characteristics" came into being and was written into central documents after Deng Xiaoping put forward the scientific topic of "taking our own path and building socialism with Chinese characteristics" at the opening ceremony of the 12th CPC National Congress. The scientific concept of the "path of socialism with Chinese characteristics" was used in the reports to the 13th and 14th CPC National Congresses as well as other important documents.

The connotation of the scientific concept is generally described and summarized at three levels. The first level is philosophical description and summary. For example, as stated in the *Report to the 14th CPC National Congress*, "We must take our own road to socialism, not regard books as dogma and not blindly copy the models of other countries. We must take Marxism as a guide to action, make practice the only test of truth, emancipate our minds, seek truth from facts, value the initiative of the people and build socialism with Chinese characteristics."[28]

The second level is description and summary based on the essence of the basic line. For example, as stated in the

Communiqué of the Seventh Plenary Session of the 13th CPC Central Committee, "Advocated by Comrade Deng Xiaoping, the Party has made a scientific judgment that China is in the primary stage of socialism, established the basic line of taking economic development as the central task and adhering to the Four Cardinal Principles, and the policy of reform and opening-up as well as a series of effective policies and guidelines made by following the principle of applying the general truths of Marxism to Chinese specific conditions and profoundly summarizing historical experience and present practical experience at the Third Plenary Session of the 11th Central Committee and the 12th and 13th CPC National Congresses. Practice has proved that the path of socialism with Chinese characteristics is a path of strengthening the country and enriching the people, and it suits China's realities."[29] For another example, the *Outline for Learning Deng Xiaoping's Theories of Building Socialism with Chinese Characteristics* compiled by the Publicity Department of the CPC Central Committee after the 14th National Congress of the Party stated, "This basic line embodies the essential requirements of socialism, reflects the fundamental law of China's socialist development and points out a development path of socialism with Chinese characteristics" on the basis of discussion of the scientific connotation of the basic line of "One Central Task and Two Basic Points."[30]

The third level is theoretical description and summary. The *Report to the 13th CPC National Congress* states, "Since the Third Plenary Session of the 11th CPC Central Committee, the Party has given full play to and developed a series of scientific theories and views on philosophy, plutonomy and scientific socialism in the process of re-understanding socialism" and points out that "these views constitute the outline of theories of socialism with Chinese characteristics, preliminarily respond to the basic issues such as stages, tasks, driving force, layout and international environment for China's socialist construction, and lay out a scientific path for our progress." [31]

For a long time, how to summarize and describe the scientific connotation of the "path of socialism with Chinese characteristics" in our theoretical research is an important topic to be studied and addressed immediately. This topic was broached at the 17th CPC National Congress, and was enriched and developed at the 18th CPC National Congress.

As defined at the 18th CPC National Congress, taking the path of socialism with Chinese characteristics means we must, under the leadership of the Communist Party of China and basing ourselves on China's realities, take economic development as the central task and adhere to the Four Cardinal Principles and the policy of reform and opening-up. It means we must release and develop the productive forces, develop the socialist market economy, socialist democracy, an advanced socialist culture and a harmonious socialist society, and promote socialist ecological progress. It also means we must promote the well-rounded development of the person, achieve prosperity for all over time, and make China a modern socialist country that is prosperous, strong, democratic, culturally advanced and harmonious.

Taking the path of socialism with Chinese characteristics means we must, under the leadership of the Communist Party of China and based on actual conditions in the primary stage of socialism, march along the basic road of "One Central Task and Two Basic Points," and advance economic, political, cultural, social and ecological progress in an all-round way to eventually promote the well-rounded development of the person and realize over time the goal of modernization characterized by prosperity for all and a prosperous, strong, democratic, culturally advanced and harmonious China.

Basic Elements of the Chinese Path

The path of socialism with Chinese characteristics has rich connotations and includes five basic elements: 1) upholding the leadership of the Communist Party of China; 2) proceeding from the actual situation that China is and will be for a long time in the primary stage of socialism; 3) adhering to the basic line of "One Central Task and Two Basic Points"; 4) following the overall plan for promoting economic, political, cultural, social and ecological progress; 5) promoting the well-rounded development of the person, achieving prosperity for all over time, and building a prosperous, strong, democratic, culturally advanced and harmonious country.

Upholding the leadership of the Communist Party of China

The scientific connotations of the path of socialism with Chinese characteristics tell us that upholding the leadership of the Party is the inherent essential condition of the path for the following reasons:

The path was proposed and adhered to by the Party, and is an unprecedented pioneering cause. The road ahead is by no means flat and we will inevitably encounter various expected and unexpected difficulties and risks from home and abroad in economic, social and political lives. To respond to and address these difficulties and risks, we need a powerful leadership core. Meanwhile, to unite more than one billion people to work hard and build socialism with Chinese characteristics, we also need a leadership core with a cohesive force and overwhelming appeal. History and reality have proved that only the Party is such a powerful leadership core.

The Party is the strong leadership core of the cause of socialism with Chinese characteristics because of its nature, purpose and political advantages. The Communist Party of China is the vanguard both of the Chinese working class and of the Chinese people and the Chinese nation as a whole. It represents the development trend of China's advanced productive forces, the orientation of China's advanced culture and the fundamental interests of the overwhelming majority of the Chinese people; it always regards serving the people wholeheartedly as its fundamental purpose and the fundamental interests of the people as the starting point and goal of all the work of the Party and country, and adheres to truths and corrects mistakes for the people. The Party adheres to the application of the basic principles of Marxism to China's specific realities to constantly propose scientific theories, action plans, guidelines and policies that can guide the development and progress of Chinese society. The Party has a broad world vision, can follow the trend of development and progress of the times, and is good at grasping historical opportunities and responding to various challenges and tests. The Party has a large number of excellent Party members who boldly strive for the people's interests and have thus won their trust and support thanks to their infinite loyalty to the people and self-sacrifice. The Party always maintains its advanced nature and purity, and strengthens its creativity, cohesiveness and capability by enhancing and improving its building work. Therefore, only under the leadership of the Party can building socialism with Chinese characteristics succeed. In this sense, the path of socialism with Chinese characteristics is a path for the Chinese people to realize social development and national rejuvenation under the Party's leadership.

Proceeding from the actual conditions of the primary stage of socialism

The scientific connotations of the path of socialism with Chinese characteristics tell us that China is and will be for a long time in the primary stage of socialism, which is the starting point and foothold of the path.

The path must be based on national conditions, and a correct path cannot be separated from China's reform and development. China is a developing country in the primary stage of socialism, during which China will gradually shake off its undeveloped state and basically realize modernization. It is the initial stage of the long historical process of socialism with Chinese characteristics. The present-stage characteristics in the new century are specific embodiments of the basic conditions of the primary stage of socialism. The basic reality that China is in the primary stage of socialism was called the overall base for socialism with Chinese characteristics at the 18th CPC National Congress. Xi Jinping said, "We emphasize the overall base because the primary stage of socialism is the biggest national condition and reality in contemporary China. We must firmly base ourselves on this reality to advance reform in all aspects. We must always bear in mind the primary stage when we promote economic, political, cultural, social and ecological progress, whether the economic aggregate is low or high, and when we plan for long-term development and do routine work."[32]

Adhering to the basic line of "One Central Task and Two Basic Points"

The scientific connotations of the path of socialism with Chinese characteristics tell us that the Party and the people must follow the basic line of "One Central Task and Two Basic Points" when building socialism with Chinese characteristics.

"One Central Task and Two Basic Points" mean we must take economic development as the central task and adhere to the Four Cardinal Principles and the policy of reform and opening-up, which form the central contents of the Party's basic line in the primary stage of socialism. This basic line, which has been established by the Party in the practice of reform and opening-up, and modernization since the Third Plenary Session of the 11th CPC Central Committee, is the only correct political line for building socialism with Chinese characteristics. The basic line is determined by the Party, by means of profoundly understanding the reality that China is in the primary stage of socialism, reflecting the basic requirements of socialist modernization in China and intensively embodying the fundamental interests and aspirations of the Chinese people of all ethnic groups.

"We must always firmly adhere to and lay an equal emphasis on the 'One Central Task and Two Basic Points' in practice, unify the common ideal of socialism with Chinese characteristics and firm lofty ideal of communism, resolutely resist various wrong views which advocate abandoning socialism, conscientiously correct reckless ideas and point out correct measures," said Xi Jinping.[33] The key to firmly adhering to the Party's basic line is to unswervingly take economic development as the central task, which is the essence of the national rejuvenation and the fundamental requirement for the prosperity and enduring peace and stability of the Party and the country. The Party's and the country's work must serve and be subordinate to the central task of economic development rather than being divorced from or interrupting it. The Four Cardinal Principles are the foundation of the country and the political cornerstone for the survival and development of the Party and the country; reform and opening-up help make China powerful, and represent the dynamic course of the Party's and the country's development and progress as well as a strong driving force to develop socialism with Chinese characteristics. Over the past 30-plus years of the reform and opening-up era we have adhered to the Party's basic line to guarantee the correct direction of reform and opening-up by means of the Four Cardinal Principles and endow these principles new connotations of the times through reform and opening-up in economic development. To adhere to this basic line in an all-round way, we must unswervingly integrate the central task of economic development and the two basic points of the Four Cardinal Principles and reform and opening-up into the great practice of building socialism with Chinese characteristics. This is the most reliable guarantee ensuring our cause will withstand all risks and tests, and march ahead. In this sense, the path of socialism with Chinese characteristics is a path for the Chinese people, under the leadership of the Party, to boldly develop socialism and realize national rejuvenation by firmly following the basic line of "One Central Task and Two Basic Points."

Following the overall plan for promoting economic, political, cultural, social and ecological progress

The scientific connotations of the path of socialism with Chinese characteristics tell us that the Party and the people must follow the overall layout of the cause of socialism with Chinese characteristics to comprehensively promote its development when following the basic line of "One Central Task and Two Basic Points."

The overall plan for the cause of socialism with Chinese characteristics means we must "promote the balanced development of socialist economic, political, cultural, social and ecological progress" to build socialism.[34]

To promote economic progress, we must take economic development as the central task, develop the socialist market economy, adhere to and improve the basic economic system in which public ownership is the mainstay and economic entities of diverse ownership develop together, as well as the income distribution system in which distribution according to work is the main form that coexists with other forms of distribution, adhere to and expand opening-up, and promote sustained and rapid economic growth. Hu Jintao emphasized at the Special Seminar for Leading Provincial Officials on July 23, 2012 that the central task of economic development is essential for reinvigorating China, and development is the key to all issues. In contemporary China, pursuing development in a scientific way best embodies the thinking that only development counts. Taking the pursuit of development in a scientific way as the underlying guideline and accelerating the change of the growth model as a major task is a strategic choice we have made for promoting China's overall development. All Party members must unify and deepen their understanding to resolutely implement the important decisions and deployments made by the central government to accelerate the change of the growth model, ensure that development is based on improved quality and performance, implement innovation-driven development strategy in a down-to-earth way, while carrying out strategic adjustment of the economic structure. It is also important to promote integrated rural and urban development and comprehensively improve the economic level of the open economy, fire all types of market participants with new vigor for development, promote harmonized development of industrialization, IT application, urbanization and agricultural modernization, and deepen economic structural reform across the board to sustain long-term development.

To promote political progress, we must build socialist democratic politics, and most importantly ensure the unity of the leadership of the Party, the position of the people as masters of the country, and law-based governance, adhere to and improve the system of people's congresses, the system of multiparty cooperation and political consultation under the leadership of the CPC, the system of regional ethnic autonomy and the system of community-level self-governance, effectively respect and safeguard human rights and expand the people's orderly participation in governance. The Party's Central Committee has emphasized that since the introduction of the reform and opening-up policies, we have always placed reform of the political structure in an important position concerning holistic reform development and unswervingly promoted the reform, thus accomplishing significant progress and successfully blazing and adhering to the socialist trail of making political advance with Chinese characteristics. To promote reform of the political structure, we must ensure the unity of the leadership of the Party, the position of the people as masters of the country, and law-based governance, to ensure that the people conduct democratic elections, decision-making, administration and oversight in accordance with the law with ever more extensive and fuller democratic rights, give greater scope to the important role the rule of law plays in the country's governance and in social management, uphold the unity, sanctity and authority of the country's legal system, and ensure that the people enjoy extensive rights and freedoms as prescribed by law.

To promote cultural progress, we must build an advanced socialist culture, and in particular strengthen the building of a harmonious culture based on the socialist core value system to better safeguard the people's basic cultural rights and interests, enrich their social and cultural lives, revitalize their spiritual outlook, develop cultural soft power and develop a strong socialist culture in China. The Party's Central Committee has emphasized that the development of a strong socialist culture in China is an important strategic decision made by the Party by grasping the changes to the times and situation and actively responding the spiritual and cultural needs of the people of all ethnic groups. We must take the socialist path of promoting cultural advance with Chinese characteristics. We should adhere to the goal of serving the people and socialism, the policy of having "a hundred flowers bloom and a hundred schools of thought contend," and the principle of maintaining close contact with reality, life and the people. We must increase our awareness of and confidence in Chinese culture, fully promote socialist cultural and ethical progress as well as material progress, and develop a national, scientific and people-oriented socialist culture that embraces modernization, the whole world and the future.

To promote social progress, we must strengthen the

focus of social construction on improving the people's well-being, basically establish a social security system in both urban and rural areas, promote social fairness and justice, strive to resolve social contradictions, build a socialist harmonious society and improve the quality of life of all the people. The Party's Central Committee stresses that to improve the people's material and cultural lives based on economic development is the fundamental purpose of the reform and opening-up and socialist modernization. Since the reform and opening-up policies were introduced, especially in the past few years, we have made great efforts and accomplished significant achievements in improving the people's well-being. At the same time, we are soberly aware that the people have increasing requirements for a better life as well as higher expectations for addressing prominent issues in the field of the people's well-being. We must continue to strengthen work in this regard, bring as much benefit as possible to the people, resolve as many difficulties as possible for them, and solve the problems of the greatest concern to them. We should keep making progress in ensuring that all the people enjoy their rights to education, remuneration for work, medical and old-age care, and housing, and enable all the people to enjoy the fruits of reform and development in a fairer way so they can lead a better life.

To promote ecological progress, we must basically establish an industrial structure, growth model and consumption model characterized by energy and resource conservation and ecological environmental protection. The Party's Central Committee has emphasized that promoting ecological progress is a strategic task involving fundamental changes to the mode of production and way of life, so we must profoundly integrate and comprehensively implement the concept, principles and goals of ecological progress in all aspects, and the whole process of China's economic, political, cultural and social progress. We must remain committed to the basic state policy of conserving resources and protecting the environment, strive for green, circular and low-carbon development, and create a sound working and living environment for the people.

Economic, political, cultural, social and ecological progress have their own tasks and priorities, depend on and promote each other, and thus constitute a unified development layout. Economic progress provides a material foundation for the other four; political progress politically guarantees the other four; cultural progress provides ideological guarantee, spiritual impetus, cultural environment and intellectual support for the other four; social progress offers the other four strong social foundations; and ecological progress provides environmental support for the other four.

Realizing the ambitious goal of building a modern socialist country that is prosperous, strong, democratic, culturally advanced and harmonious while promoting all-round development of the person and achieving prosperity for all over time

The scientific connotations of the path of socialism with Chinese characteristics tell us we must adopt a holistic approach to promote the all-round development of the person, achieve prosperity for all over time and focus on the four goals of prosperity, democracy, advanced culture and harmony to comprehensively promote the development of the cause of socialism with Chinese characteristics by stages.

At the present stage, the development goals of socialism with Chinese characteristics are, under the leadership of the Party and through the hard work of the people of all ethnic groups, to promote the all-round development of the person, achieve prosperity for all over time and turn China into a modern socialist country that is prosperous, strong, democratic, culturally advanced and harmonious.

To realize these goals we must implement development strategies by stages and by steps in a scientific way. In the early stage of reform and opening-up, Deng Xiaoping designed an ambitious blueprint of modernization by "three steps."[35]

At the end of the 20th century when China was going to realize the second-step strategic goal, the Party further made a plan for the realization of the third-step strategic goal at the 15th CPC National Congress, and clearly stated the development goal of "three small steps."[36] In the 21st century, the 16th CPC National Congress established the goal of building a moderately prosperous society in all respects by 2020. In other words, after arduous efforts of 20 years we will have built a moderately prosperous society that will benefit all the Chinese people and will be characterized by faster economic growth, more complete democracy, more advanced science and education, more prosperous culture, more harmonious society and the people's well-being. By then, China will have become a country that has basically realized industrialization, significantly improved its comprehensive national strength and ranks among leading countries by domestic market size. It will also be a country that generally increases the people's affluence, significantly improves the people's quality of life and fosters a good ecological environment — a country in which the people enjoy fuller democratic rights and have a higher cultural quality and spiritual pursuits, that boasts more sophisticated systems, more dynamism, stability and unity, that opens wider to the outside world, is more amicable and makes great contributions to mankind.

Therefore, to realize the great rejuvenation of the Chinese nation, we must take the path of socialism with Chinese characteristics. That means we must, under the Party's leadership and based on the reality that China is in the primary stage of socialism, boldly proceed along the basic line of "One Central Task and Two Basic Points," comprehensively implement the overall plan for promoting economic, political, cultural, social and ecological progress, promote well-rounded development of the person by stages and by steps, achieve prosperity for all over time and make China a modern socialist country that is prosperous, strong, democratic, culturally advanced and harmonious.

Not a Capitalist Path with Chinese Characteristics

Based on an analysis of the scientific connotations of the path of socialism with Chinese characteristics, we clearly see that the path of socialism with Chinese characteristics is a product of a combination of the basic principles of scientific socialism with China's practices and characteristics of the times. As General Secretary Xi Jinping put it, "Socialism with Chinese characteristics is socialism and nothing else."[37]

In other words, the path of socialism with Chinese characteristics is not a "path of capitalism with Chinese characteristics" or "path of state capitalism" as some said.

Of course, analysis is necessary to address this issue:

Why do some people argue that socialism with Chinese
characteristics is "capitalism with Chinese characteristics" or
"state capitalism"? I have noticed that such a misunderstanding is mainly caused by some social phenomena. The following
four aspects are especially noticeable:

First, we have decided in our economic structural reform
to replace the old planned economy with a socialist market
economy and develop our economy with different types of
ownership, including individual economy and private economy
to replace the single form of public ownership economy and
reform the state-owned economy by a shareholding system.
Many people both at home and abroad believe the essence of
such a transformation of the economic system is to replace socialism with capitalism.

Second, as we adhere to reform and constantly open wider
to the outside world, more and more foreign capital has entered the Chinese market.

Third, the reform and opening-up process have seen a rise
in egoism, money worship, hedonism and other negative ideas
and degenerate lifestyle, resulting in frequent cases of official

corruption.

Fourth, while developing market economy, China has never given up macro control over national economy. In particular, in respond to the international financial crisis, the Chinese government has intensified effort in macro control, thus triggering off the topic of so-called "state capitalism."

Therefore, many people believe socialism with Chinese characteristics is "capitalism with Chinese characteristics" or "state capitalism."

However, we must analyze these phenomena instead of lumping them together.

The emergence of egoism, money worship, hedonism and other negative ideas and degenerate lifestyles, including official corruption, calls for great concern. However, there are very complicated reasons behind these problems which are prohibited by the Party's disciplines and the country's laws. Hence we cannot assert that socialism with Chinese characteristics is capitalism with Chinese characteristics, because of these problems in real life.

Deng Xiaoping clearly stated that the market economy and shareholding system are methods which can be leveraged by both capitalist and socialist countries, and reflect the development law of modern society. What Deng Xiaoping said is right and reflects the objective reality of the world's economic development since World War II. Therefore, we cannot assert that socialism with Chinese characteristics is capitalism with Chinese characteristics because China chose a socialist market economic system and shareholding system in the course of reform and opening-up.

As to the issue of developing individual and private economies, and introducing foreign capital, we must realize that no society is pure, and be aware of the dominant economy, politics and ideology of our society as well as the characteristics of these economic and social phenomena. The existence and development of these economic forms are determined by China's reality that China is in the primary stage of socialism and are bounded by basic socialist systems and laws, thus differing from the many forms of private economy in the past. In particular, those economic forms by no means entirely belonged to the capitalist economy in the past in consideration of their original capital source, characteristics of operational process, internal labor relations of enterprises, distribution of surplus value and contributions to social employment, national economic growth and tax revenue. Therefore, we cannot assert that socialism with Chinese characteristics is capitalism with Chinese characteristics, because China implements an economic system in which public ownership is the mainstay and economic entities of diverse ownership develop together.

As for whether China implements "state capitalism" because it exercises macro control over the economy, we reply that many countries exercise macro control over their national economy mainly by using economic, legal and administrative means, especially since World War II. In response to the international financial crisis, the Chinese government promulgated a whole package of economic incentive measures and intensified efforts in the areas of macro control and administrative regulation in particular. After these special measures in the special period had played their roles, the Chinese government promptly proposed to correctly handle the relationship between the government and the market. China's macro control is no longer the same as the planned economy in the past. Our national economy and deepening institutional reform differ from those in the era of the planned economy, and our national economy competes with economies of other ownerships within the socialist market system (we are now further addressing the fairness of such competition). Therefore, it is irrational to claim that China implements "state capitalism" because we have strengthened macro control over the national economy.

In a word, socialism with Chinese characteristics is scientific socialism on a theoretical basis of scientific socialism, and its theories and institutional design embody the developments of Marxism. Hence socialism with Chinese characteristics is scientific socialism based on China's reality that this country is in the primary stage of socialism.

Chinese Path in the Course of Economic and Social Development

Path of Independent Innovation with Chinese Characteristics

New Path of Industrialization with Chinese Characteristics

Path of Agricultural Modernization with Chinese Characteristics

Path of Urbanization with Chinese Characteristics

Chinese Path:
Economic and Social Development

"The path of socialism with Chinese characteristics is an overall road for China's development that is composed of numerous specific paths. The 17th CPC National Congress put forward the path of independent innovation with Chinese characteristics, new path of industrialization with Chinese characteristics, path of urbanization with Chinese characteristics, path of political development under socialism with Chinese characteristics, path of combating corruption and upholding integrity with Chinese characteristics, etc. We must continue to explore and develop these specific paths with new practices so as to constantly enrich and develop the overall path of socialism with Chinese characteristics."[38] This statement by Hu Jintao indicates that the Party proposes that we must firmly march along the path of socialism with Chinese characteristics, and explore and adhere to specific paths in the economic, political, cultural and social fields.

Chinese Path in the Course of Economic and Social Development

Taking the path of socialism with Chinese characteristics is a general task which requires us to further research specific conditions for and significant issues to be addressed for China's economic and social development.

Our ultimate goal of taking the path of socialism with Chinese characteristics is to "make China a modern socialist country that is prosperous, strong, democratic, culturally advanced and harmonious, with the starting point of the reality that China is a developing socialist country in the primary stage of socialism. The 13th CPC National Congress described China's basic conditions as follows:

How do things stand in China, now that socialism has been developing here for more than three decades? On the one hand, a socialist economic system based on public ownership of the means of production has been instituted, a socialist political system of people's democratic dictatorship has been established, and the guiding role of Marxism in the realm of ideology has been affirmed. The system of exploitation and the exploiting classes have been abolished. China's economic strength has grown enormously, and educational, scientific and cultural undertakings have considerably expanded. On the other hand, the country has a huge population and had a poor economic foundation to start with, and its per capita GNP still ranks among the lowest in the world. The picture is very clear: Out of a population of more than one billion, 800 million people live in rural areas and, for the most part, still use hand tools to make a living. A certain number of modern industries coexist with many industries that are several decades or even a century behind present-day standards. Some areas that are fairly developed economically coexist with vast areas that are underdeveloped and impoverished. A small amount of science and technology is up to the highest world standards while the scientific and technological level as a whole is low, and nearly one-quarter of the population is still illiterate or semi-literate. The backwardness of the productive forces determines the following aspects of the relations of production: The socialization of production, which is essential for expanded socialist public ownership, is still at a very low level; the commodity economy and domestic market are only beginning to develop; the natural economy and semi-natural economy constitute a considerable proportion of the whole; and the socialist economic system is not yet mature. In the realm of the superstructure, a number of economic and cultural conditions that are necessary if we are to promote a high degree of socialist democracy are far from ripe, and decadent feudal and capitalist ideologies and the small-producers' force of habit still have widespread influence in society and often corrode Party officials and public servants. All this shows that we still have a long way to go before we can advance beyond the primary stage of socialism.[39]

Great changes have taken place in China since 1987, when the 13th CPC National Congress was convened. In particular, as China has established a socialist market economic system and fully participated in economic globalization, it has accomplished great progress in economy, politics, culture and comprehensive national strength, but it is generally still in the primary stage of socialism. Particularly, in the economic and social fields, China's per capita GNP still ranks among the lowest in the world. Backward agriculture, backward rural areas and poor farmers remain bottlenecks in the course of China's modernization. Some areas that are fairly well developed economically coexist with vast areas that are underdeveloped and impoverished. China has not realized industrialization yet and faces the challenge of IT application. Science and technology not yet applied to economic development and low capacity in scientific and technological innovation are problems yet to be addressed. Such basic conditions impose a severe challenge on China in its efforts to realize socialist modernization.

Targeting these problems, the Party's Central Committee believes that to pursue the path of socialism with Chinese characteristics we must make an overall plan for industrialization, IT application, urbanization and agricultural modernization in the economic and social fields and take the path of independent innovation with Chinese characteristics, the new path of industrialization with Chinese characteristic and the path of urbanization with Chinese characteristics. As emphasized by the 18th CPC National Congress, "We should keep to the Chinese-style path of carrying out industrialization in a new way and advancing IT application, urbanization and agricultural modernization. We should promote the integration of IT application and industrialization, interaction between industrialization and urbanization, and coordination between urbanization and agricultural modernization, thus promoting the harmonized development of industrialization, IT application, urbanization and agricultural modernization."[40]

Path of Independent Innovation with Chinese Characteristics

As clearly stated in the *Report to the 18th CPC National Congress*, when "implementing the strategy of innovation-driven development" was expounded, "We should follow the path of making innovation with Chinese features and take steps to promote innovation to catch up with global advances. We should increase our capacity for making original innovations and integrated innovations, and for making further innovations on the basis of absorbing advances in overseas science and technology, and place greater emphasis on making innovations through collaboration."[41] Scientific and technological innovation is a strategic support to the social productive forces and comprehensive national strength. Taking the path of independent innovation with Chinese characteristics, improving our capability for independent innovation and turning China into an innovation-oriented country represent the core of the national development strategy laid down by the CPC, and the key factor for improving comprehensive national strength.

First, why does China have to improve its capacity for independent innovation?

Since the 1970s science and technology have advanced rapidly on a global scale, and a new round of scientific and technological revolution has developed by leaps and bounds. With advancing economic globalization, scientific and technological development exerts a powerful influence on a country's comprehensive national strength and international standing in an extensive and profound way that has never been seen before. Many countries regard scientific and technological innovation as a national development strategy, and compete to seize the commanding height of international competition in comprehensive national strength. China also faces an imperative task of independent innovation in order to accelerate the change of its growth model, optimize and upgrade its industrial structure, strengthen its energy and resource conservation and ecological environmental protection, and safeguard its national security. In particular, China faces high-pressure competition in the field of comprehensive national strength. On the one hand, we face the opportunities and challenges of the new scientific and technological revolution and economic globalization, taking into account the fact that the developed countries have been in the dominant position in economy and science and technology for a long time, and face real domestic demands for economic and social development. On the other hand, some developed countries refuse to allow advanced core technologies to be sold to China under various pretexts, despite the fact that we are opening wider to the outside world. Therefore, we must follow the development trend of the times and meet development needs to change the situation of advanced core technology controlled by others and improve China's capacity for independent innovation.

Second, does China have the conditions to improve its capacity for independent innovation?

China has built a foundation for innovation in science and technology. Thanks to the concerted efforts of the country and Chinese scientists and engineers since the founding of New China in 1949, and the reform and opening-up policies in particular, China has built a complete discipline system and made great achievements in basic research, research into cutting-edge technology, research into market-oriented application and development, research into significant scientific programs. In particular, China has realized the ambitious dream of "being capable of reaching the moon and catching turtles deep in the ocean" thanks to the rapid development of its aerospace sector and breakthroughs in research into manned submersibles. Our achievements and experience in various disciplines of science and technology have laid a solid foundation for further promoting scientific and technological innovation. Moreover, China has rich human resources in science and technology, numbering 35 million persons and ranking first in the world. China's 1.5 million R&D staff members rank in the second place in the world, and the total number of students at institutions of higher learning exceeds 23 million. These rich human resources provide a strong scientific research force and a talent reserve for independent innovation, and represent China's biggest advantage in taking the path of independent innovation. In addition, China has established an industrial system characterized by a wide variety of products and strong supporting capacity, built a group of science and technology parks, scientific research bases and high-tech enterprises that are characterized by close integration of economy with science and technology, and made numerous top-notch scientific and technological achievements.

For example, leading science and technology parks include the Zhongguancun National Independent Innovation Demonstration Zone in Beijing and the Zhangjiang National Independent Innovation Demonstration Zone in Pudong,

Shanghai; leading science and technology bases include the Hybrid Rice Test Base presided over by Yuan Longping known as the Father of Hybrid Rice; and leading high-tech enterprises include Lenovo in Beijing and Huawei in Shenzhen.

In particular, we also have advantages in system and spirit. In terms of system, we can mobilize and integrate resources to accomplish great undertakings, focus on making breakthroughs and realize development based on the great demand for national economic and social development. Moreover, we can also give full play to the basic role of the market in resource allocation, make scientific and technological innovations serve the national will and strategic goals, and abide by the laws of the socialist market economy, fully arousing the enthusiasm and creativity of all innovation participants. In terms of spirit, China has developed a valuable spirit of independent innovation. The spirit of "two bombs and one satellite," which took shape in tough conditions in the early days of New China, and the spirit of "manned space flight," which took shape in the course of reform and opening-up, indicate that Chinese scientists and engineers and the Chinese people as a whole have a strong spirit of independent innovation that has already become an important symbol of China's national spirit and the spirit of the times. These advantages provide important conditions for us to improve our capacity for independent innovation, grasp the initiative of development and create new advantages for development.

What is and how can we follow the path of independent innovation with Chinese characteristics?

On June 23, 2008 Hu Jintao delivered a speech at the 14th General Assembly of the Chinese Academy of Sciences (CAS) and the 9th General Assembly of the Chinese Academy of Engineering (CAE), putting forward four requirements for taking the path of independent innovation with Chinese characteristics:[42]

First, to take the path of independent innovation with Chinese characteristics, we must regard improving our capability of independent innovation as the primary task of scientific and technological development. This is a strategic guideline for turning China into an innovation-oriented country. Hu said we must give top priority to innovative sci-tech work to improve our capability of independent innovation, conscientiously implement the Outline of the National Medium- and Long-term Plan for Scientific and Technological Development, accelerate the organization and implementation of important national special sci-tech projects, increase investment in independent innovation, arouse vitality for innovation and strengthen the driving force for innovation. Moreover, we must vigorously promote original innovation, integrated innovation as well as re-innovation based on introduction and absorption; focus on breakthroughs in key technologies that constrain economic and social development; and support basic research, research into cutting-edge technologies and research into social public welfare technologies. We should master core technologies in several important fields, develop a number of independent intellectual property rights, establish a group of enterprises with international competitiveness and create a large number of leading international brands that are high value-added and have core intellectual property rights.

We must also attach great importance to integration among basic disciplines, between basic disciplines and applied disciplines, between science and technology as well as between natural science and humanistic and social science, accurately know the main characteristics of development of frontier science and technology such as unity of microscopic view and macroscopic view and the combination of reductionism and holism, make an overall plan for basic and applied disciplines, promote significant improvement in innovation capacity and facilitate balanced development of multiple disciplines in multiple fields. We must make putting people first and improving the people's well-being the fundamental starting point and goal of scientific and technological development so that all people will benefit from the fruits of scientific and technological progress and innovation. We must build several world-class scientific research institutes and universities as well as enterprise R&D

institutions with international competitiveness and accelerate the building of a national innovation system to strike a balance among the technological innovation, knowledge innovation, defense-related science and technology innovation, regional innovation and scientific and technological intermediary service systems. We must follow the basic national policy of opening-up, expand international and regional scientific and technological exchanges and cooperation in diverse forms, conscientiously learn and fully absorb international advanced scientific and technological achievements, and make full use of global science and technology resources.

Second, to take the path of independent innovation with Chinese characteristics we must promote scientific and technological progress and innovation by means of an institutional system. Hu said it is imperative to renovate our systems and mechanisms so as to drive scientific and technological progress and innovation and improve our capacity for independent innovation. We must make serving national objectives and mobilizing the enthusiasm and creativity of all scientific and technological personnel as the starting point, and focus on facilitating the high-efficiency allocation and comprehensive integration of all scientific and technological resources. This should be achieved by accelerating the establishment of a market-oriented technological innovation system in which enterprises are the main participants and which is characterized by a combination of industry, higher education and research. In the building of a national innovation system, we must deepen reform of the science and technology system and various supporting reforms to form dynamic systems and mechanisms that help promote scientific and technological progress and innovation, help facilitate the translation of scientific and technological achievements into real productive forces, embody Chinese characteristics and meet the laws of scientific and technological development. We must establish and complete the national scientific and technological decision-making mechanism and macro coordination system, strengthen overall planning for important scientific and technological decision making, implementation of significant scientific and technological programs and construction of scientific and technological infrastructures, accelerate the layout and structural adjustment of scientific research, reform scientific and technological achievement evaluation and reward systems, and promote the effective allocation of scientific and technological resources.

Third, to take the path of independent innovation with Chinese characteristics we must build a large contingent of innovative personnel, as it directly concerns the future of China's science and technology as well as that of the country and the nation. Outstanding scientists and sci-tech personnel determine the development of national science and technology. We must regard human resource as the first resource, comprehensively implement the strategy of making China strong by training competent personnel, adopt policy measures conducive to their growth based on the requirement of promoting all-round development of the person, and foster systems, mechanisms and an environment that help such personnel mature and play their roles. We must follow the growth law of innovative scientific and technological personnel, extensively absorb talents, discover and make use of talents in innovation practices, train and exercise talents in innovation activities, and gather together and reward talented people in the cause of innovation. We must improve and complete the professional title system, academician system, special government allowance system, postdoctoral system and other high-level personnel systems, and optimize the project investment system and structure to form systems and mechanisms that highlight excellent talent. We must give priority to education development, update our education concept, deepen educational reform and innovation, promote quality-oriented education in an all-round way, adjust the structures of disciplines and majors, and innovate a personnel training model. We must intensify efforts to introduce talented people and improve expertise introduction work and, in particular, actively introduce overseas high-caliber personnel and intelligence and attract overseas Chinese students to return to China.

Fourth, to take the path of independent innovation with Chinese characteristics we must encourage scientific and technological progress and innovation with an innovative culture. Cultural inheritance and development is of vital importance to scientific and technological progress and innovation. We must vigorously foster China's national characteristics with patriotism at the core and promote the underlying trends of the times with reform and innovation at the core, uphold love for the motherland, selfless contribution, self-dependence and hard struggle as well as the collaborative and bold spirit encapsulated in the expression "two bombs and one satellite," carry forward the spirit of the manned spaceflight program of being particularly good at withstanding extraordinary hardships, being particularly good at fighting hard battles and tackling technological problems with great dedication, and advocate a reforming, innovative and boldly enterprising spirit. We must spare no efforts to encourage and support scientific and technological innovation, arouse the enthusiasm and vitality of scientific and technological personnel for innovation, encourage, support and help talented people to dedicate themselves to the cause, and in particular provide more opportunities and a bigger stage for young professionals to give full play to their talents, and foster a favorable social atmosphere that respects and encourages innovation and entrepreneurship.

The National Conference on Science and Technology Innovation held on July 6-7, 2012 in Beijing laid down our goals for improv-ing our capacity for independent innovation and turning China into an innovation-based country by 2020. According to the conference, by 2020 we will realize the following goals: basically build a national innovation system with Chinese characteristics that suits the socialist market economic system and meets the development law of science and technology; significantly improve our capacity for original innovation; considerably enhance our capacity for integrated innovation and re-innovation based on introduction and absorption; make significant breakthroughs in scientific research in key fields, realize cutting-edge development of technological research and development in strategic high-tech fields and rank as one of leading countries in the world in the sphere of innovation achievements in several fields. At the same time, we will optimize the environment for innovation, significantly improve innovation efficiency, train numerous innovative professionals, make the whole nation better educated in science, considerably improve the capacity of science and technology for supporting and leading economic and social development, and enter the ranks of the innovation-based countries. [43]

New Path of Industrialization with Chinese Characteristics

Those who are familiar with the formation and development of Marxism know that industrialization is directly related to scientific socialism. Industrialization as the development of socialized mass production represents an important social condition for the formation and development of scientific socialism. Socialism and communism are built in the process of resolving the basic contradiction in capitalist society – that between socialized production and capitalist private ownership based on the requirements of socialized mass production and its representative working class. As China is an economically and culturally backward country, the process of establishing and building socialism is closely related to the process of industrialization.

In consideration of the close relationship between industrialization and socialism, what path China takes to realize industrialization will inevitably influence the path of socialism chosen by China and vice versa. Actually, China put forward the issue of the path of industrialization with Chinese characteristics in the mid-1950s, and it was explored and discussed by Mao Zedong in his *On the Ten Major Relationships* and *On the Correct Handling of Contradictions among the People*. The focus at that time was that to realize industrialization China could not simply follow the path of industrialization of developing heavy industry at the cost of agriculture and light industry that was taken by the Soviet Union. Mao said, "The issue of the path of industrialization that I mention mainly refers to the development relationship among heavy industry, light industry and agriculture. We must be sure that China's economic development is centered on heavy industry, but we must also give full attention to developing agriculture and light industry."[44] This path of industrialization put forward by Mao Zedong was the path of socialism with Chinese characteristics, which was different from the Soviet Union's experience and a remarkable proposal at that time. However, we must be aware that it was impossible for China to break away from traditional industrialization under the then historical conditions.

After the introduction of the reform and opening-up policies the Party members represented by Deng Xiaoping further pondered the issue. "For economic development, we must take a Chinese-style path of modernization,"[45] Deng pointed out at the Party's Theoretical Work Discussion Meeting in March 1979. He added at the 13th CPC National Congress in October 1987: "In the primary stage of socialism, the historical issue to be addressed for developing the social productive forces is to realize industrialization and commoditized, socialized and modernized production. China's economic development undertakes dual tasks — focusing on promoting the traditional industrial revolution and catching up with the new global technological revolution." The dual tasks indicate that China was forming a new idea of industrialization with Chinese characteristics that went beyond traditional industrialization and embodied the new features of the times. China proposed the important thought of "taking the new path of industrialization" in tune with the rapid development of IT application on a global scale at the 16th CPC National Congress in November 2002. As Jiang Zemin put it in the *Report to the 16th CPC National Congress*, "It remains an arduous historical task in the process of our modernization drive to accomplish industrialization. IT application is a logical choice if the industrialization and modernization of our country are to be accelerated. It is, therefore, necessary to persist in using IT to propel industrialization, which will, in turn, stimulate IT application, blazing a new trail to industrialization featuring high scientific and technological contents, good economic returns, low resources consumption, minimal environmental pollution and a full display of advantages in human resources."[46]

Compared with traditional industrialization, the "new path of industrialization" put forward at the 16th CPC National Congress is new in the following three aspects: First, the developed countries promoted IT application after industrialization. China is a developing country, but it has witnessed rapid IT application development in recent years. As a result, China can promote IT application in the process of industrialization, and persist in using IT to propel industrialization, which will, in turn, stimulate IT application so as to realize leapfrog development of the productive forces. Second, most developed countries accomplished industrialization at the cost of energy consumption and environmental degradation, in the rapid development period in particular, resulting in far-reaching negative effects. In the process of industrialization, we must pay special attention to ecological progress and environmental protection and emphasize striking a balance between economic development and population, resources and the environment. Third, the developed countries focused on mechanization and automation to accomplish industrialization, resulting in an unemployment problem. China has a large population and very low labor cost. Hence we must strike a balance between capital- and technology-intensive industry and labor-intensive industry, between high-tech industry and traditional industry, as well as between the real economy and the virtual economy to purposefully expand employment while accomplishing industrialization. Obviously, this new path of industrialization calls on us to summarize our own experience as well as the lessons in industrialization of other countries, on the basis of China's national conditions and according to requirements and favorable conditions for realizing industrialization in the information age. This approach will certainly play a positive role in accelerating industrialization and modernization in China.

The 17th CPC National Congress convened in October 2007 summarized China's practices and experience in exploring the "path of socialism with Chinese characteristics" and the "new path of industrialization" over the past 50-plus years and made a historical decision to "keep to the new path of industrialization with Chinese characteristics," to adhere to scientific development, accelerate the transformation of the development pattern and promote industrial structure optimization and upgrading.

To profoundly understand the Party's idea and decision to "keep to the new path of industrialization with Chinese characteristics", we must first understand the current situation of industrialization in China as well as the Party's requirements for the new path of industrialization with Chinese characteristics.

The *Report to the 16th CPC National Congress* set out the strategic task of "building a well-off society in an all-round way" and announced that China would "basically accomplish industrialization by 2020."[47] This means China will become an industrialized country despite missing the historical opportunity of the Industrial Revolution and after great efforts of 180 years since the First Opium War of 1840.

Experts at the Economic Forecast Department of the State Information Center once used a forecast model to predict that China would complete the middle stage of industrialization in 2014 and enter the later stage of industrialization in 2015, based on an analysis of China's macro policies, industrial structure adjustments, population and other exogenous economic variables as well as world economic conditions in the 12th Five-year Plan period (2011-2015). Based on the measurement criteria for the industrialization index, they figured out China's comprehensive industrialization index in the late stage of the 12th Five-year Plan (2015) at 84.7, and forecast that China would then enter the later stage of industrialization as a whole. The urbanization index would be 75.6, putting China at the end of the middle stage of industrialization; the output proportion index of tertiary industry would be 88, entering the later stage of industrialization; the employment proportion index of tertiary industry would be 81.3, just entering the later stage of industrialization; and the per capita GDP index would be 86.6, fully entering the later stage of industrialization.

Experts agreed with the Economic Forecast Department of the State Information Center that China had already entered the transition period from the middle stage to the later stage of industrialization when the 11th Five-year Plan (2006-2010) was completed, and is expected to accomplish industrialization by 2020.

History and reality tell us that industrialization is a historical process shared by all countries in the world, and a special historical course for each nation. China has a population of 1.3 billion, so to realize industrialization it must learn and draw ideas from the experiences of countries which have accomplished industrialization. China greatly differs from countries which have accomplished industrialization in population size, resource endowment and history, so we must take the new path of industrialization with Chinese characteristics instead of following the paths taken by other countries. The new path of industrialization with Chinese characteristics adopts shared characteristics of industrialization of other countries, together with Chinese characteristics and advantages in today's world. The Party's Central Committee has put forward a series of important requirements for the new path of industrialization with Chinese characteristics.

First, we must pursue development in a scientific way by accelerating the change of the growth model. Historically, the industrialization of developed countries was accompanied by class exploitation or colonial spoliation at the cost of large-scale resource consumption and environmental damage which are typically characterized by the catchwords "sheep devour men" and "pollution first and treatment later." China's traditional path of industrialization was also characterized by extensive growth, prominent structural contradictions and unsustainable development. To promote industrialization, we must review the path of industrialization based on the Scientific Outlook on Development. As pointed out in the *Report to the 17th CPC National Congress*, when thoroughly applying the Scientific Outlook on Development, accelerating the transformation of the mode of economic development and upgrading the industrial structure are pressing strategic tasks vital to the national economy as a whole. We must keep to the new path of industrialization with Chinese characteristics, pursue the policy of boosting domestic demand, particularly consumer demand, and propel three transitions in the mode of economic growth: the transition from relying mainly on investment and exports to relying on a well coordinated combination of consumption, investment and export; the transition from secondary industry serving as the major driving farce to primary, secondary and tertiary industries jointly driving economic growth; and the transition from relying heavily on increased consumption of material resources to relying mainly on advances in science and technology, improvement in the quality of the workforce and innovation in management. Therefore, the new path of industrialization with Chinese characteristics means we must accelerate the change of the growth model and pursue development in a scientific way. We must adopt an enlightened approach to development that results in expanded production, a better life and sound ecological and environmental conditions, place more emphasis on building a resource-conserving and environmentally-friendly society that coordinates growth rate with the economic structure, quality and efficiency, and harmonizes economic growth with the population, resources and environment, so that we can realize economic and social development in a scientific, harmonious and sustainable way.

Second, we must concentrate on independent innovation and target the combination of industrialization and IT application. The developed capitalist countries industrialized by being driven by the Scientific and Technological Revolution and in the development course of the Scientific and Technological Revolution, which is a significant reference for China to accomplish its own industrialization. China's traditional path of industrialization was characterized by extensive growth, inadequate technological innovation and high dependence on foreign technology, so improving our capacity for scientific and technological innovation becomes an imperative task for China. To keep to the new path of independent innovation with Chinese characteristics we must take improving our capacity for independent innovation as the strategic basis of industrialization and the central link of industrial structure optimization and upgrading, constantly improve the overall technological level and core competitiveness, and turn China into a big industrial power.

Third, we must integrate industrialization with urbanization and marketization and take industrial structural adjustment and industrial layout optimization as the central link. China's industrialization today is developing amidst mutual connections and mutual promotion with IT application, urbanization, marketization and internationalization. Such an integration and connection are necessitated by the fact that China's process of industrialization is the process of rural workers migrating into cities and villages being upgraded to towns, as well as the process of optimized resource allocation by the market. Therefore, we must attach great importance to the transfer of the rural labor force and take a long-term approach based on reality to establish pension and medical security systems for migrant rural workers in cities to free them from worries. However, the fundamental way to address the problem is to take the path of urbanization with Chinese characteristics, encourage and guide industries to concentrate themselves in small and medium-sized cities and towns, and encourage and guide the transfer of surplus rural labor from the rural areas to small and medium-sized cities and towns.

Fourth, we must take increasing consumer demand as support, and reforming and opening-up as the driving forces. In the early stage of reform and opening-up, China's industrialization was based on an economy driven by investment and exports, but it was difficult to maintain such an economic growth and expansion model. The Party was soberly aware before the 17th CPC National Congress that excess capacity as a result of investment expansion and increasing dependence on foreign trade had greatly increased the uncertainties and potential risks accompanying China's economic growth. As a result, the Party proposed that we should accelerate the change of the pattern of industrial development, take the new path of industrialization with Chinese characteristics, combine industrialization with expansion of domestic demand and domestic consumer demand in particular, and firmly pursue industrial development on the basis of the expansion of domestic market to provide strong support for the steady advance of industrialization and provide a fundamental guarantee for its sustainable development. To this end, in the process of accomplishing industrialization we must strike a balance between production and consumption as well as between accumulation and consumption, actively promote and expand employment, make every effort to increase individual incomes, improve education, and the medical and pension security systems to reduce pressures on ordinary people and give full play to the role played by consumption in driving national economic and industrial growth.

Path of Agricultural Modernization with Chinese Characteristics

Agriculture is the foundation of the national economy, and national modernization depends on agricultural modernization. This is an objective law that has been repeatedly proved in the history of civilization and in the history of China as a developing country with a large population. Turning China from a backward agricultural country into an advanced industrial country is an objective of the struggle put forward by the Party when New China was founded over six decades ago. However, how to improve agricultural modernization instead of damaging agricultural development represents a difficult task to be addressed by the Party in the process of industrialization. International experience has proved that balanced development between industry and agriculture and between the urban and the rural areas is an important precondition for successful modernization.

In the new century China has rapidly advanced toward becoming an industrialized, information-based, urbanized, market-oriented and internationalized country in a profound and extensive way. China faces challenges of industrialization and urbanization in particular for agricultural development as well as good opportunities for the accelerated modernization of agriculture. Against such a backdrop, the *Report to the 17th CPC National Congress* explicitly stated that "we will strengthen the position of agriculture as the foundation of the national economy and take a path of agricultural modernization with Chinese characteristics."[48]

Since the introduction of the reform and opening-up policies, China has rapidly advanced its industrialization, and its agricultural productivity has also been greatly unleashed in the reform of the rural economic system. However, China has a large population and relatively scarce per capita agricultural natural resources such as farmland, so China generally lags behind other countries in its conditions for and means of agricultural production. At present, China faces increasingly severe challenges concerning agricultural production, including diminishing agricultural acreage, shortage of fresh water resources, serious aging and disrepair of farmland water-conservancy facilities and backward development of agricultural science and technology. The output of over half of China's cultivated land depends on the weather and over 35 billion kg of grain are lost due to natural disasters every year. As a result, food and major agricultural products are in a tight balance between demand and supply under normal conditions, and China needs to import several agricultural products. Meanwhile, with economic and social development and improved people's livelihood, the demand for agricultural products keeps increasing and agriculture faces increasing pressure. By summarizing the practices and experience since the reform and opening-up era began, the Party's Central Committee takes addressing rural issues concerning agriculture, the countryside and farmers as a top priority to realize modernization in China. Practice has taught us that only by following the universal law of world agricultural development, based on China's realities, accelerating agricultural modernization and realizing sustainable and steady agricultural development can we meet the requirements of building a moderately prosperous society in all respects and keep the momentum of the modernization of the whole country.

What is and how can we blaze the trail of agricultural modernization with Chinese characteristics?

When exploring this issue, the Party reiterated that to keep to the path of agricultural modernization with Chinese characteristics, we must base ourselves on China's realities, and take building a new socialist countryside as a strategic task and balancing urban and rural economic and social development as a fundamental requirement. Meanwhile, we must continue to encourage industry to support agriculture in return for agriculture's earlier contribution to the development of industry, and encourage the cities to support the rural areas. We should give more to farmers, take less from them, and lift restrictions on their economic activities to promote sound yet rapid economic and social development in the rural areas. This is the general guideline for the path of agricultural modernization with Chinese characteristics as determined by the Central Committee.

We should speed up the development of modern agriculture, develop agricultural science and technology and raise the overall production capacity of agriculture. Moreover, we should better balance urban and rural development, comprehensively deepen rural reform and boost rural development.

To speed up the development of modern agriculture and develop agricultural science and technology we should streamline services to agricultural science and technology and raise the overall production capacity of agriculture, which is an important task of agricultural modernization, a necessary condition for food security and the effective supply of major agricultural products, and an important driving force to change backward agriculture and promote agricultural modernization.

To better balance urban and rural development, comprehensively deepen rural reform and boost rural development, we should remove economic and political barriers standing in the way of the development of the rural productive forces, including actively and prudently advancing reform of township institutions. We should deepen overall rural reform, expand the coverage of public finance in rural areas and strengthen public services in rural areas. Moreover, we should promote orderly land transfer under collective ownership and advance reform of the tenure of collective forests. We should actively and prudently carry forward reform and innovation in the financial system in the rural areas, accelerate the improvement of integrated urban and rural systems and mechanisms, enlarge the employment space for farmers, and offer farmers more job opportunities through multiple channels to increase their incomes and reduce their burdens. These systematic and institutional reforms and innovations can provide an institutional guarantee for advancing agricultural modernization and building a new socialist countryside in a down-to-earth way.

Advancing urbanization and new countryside building in parallel represent two most important measures to create a new situation of integrated urban and rural economic and social development. The transfer of rural residents to cities will be an inexhaustible motive force behind sustained yet rapid economic growth based on domestic demand expansion in decades to come in China, and will also entail urbanization facing enormous pressures to expand employment, increase housing and improve the social security system for many years to come. At the same time, we must be soberly aware that China's population is one billion more than the USA's and as much as 10 times that of Japan. In the foreseeable future it will be impossible for China to accomplish basic population urbanization like the USA and Japan.

Hundreds of millions of Chinese people will still live in rural areas for many years to come, which is an unavoidable fact. Therefore, while actively promoting urbanization, we must steadily advance the building of a new socialist countryside, constantly improve production and living conditions in rural areas, gradually improve farmers' overall quality and create the proper conditions for the development of modern agriculture in accordance with the overall requirements of "production development, well-off life, civilized village atmosphere, clean villages and democratic management."

We believe we will certainly blaze a trail of agricultural modernization with Chinese characteristics and promote the development of the cause of socialism with Chinese characteristics, as long as we unswervingly proceed from China's realities in the rural areas and farmers' fundamental interests to deepen reforms in the rural economic system and related systems, and develop modern agriculture.

Path of Urbanization with Chinese Characteristics

"Urbanization in China and the high-tech development in America are two critical factors impacting human development in the 21st Century," said Joseph E. Stiglitz, Nobel Economics Prize winner and former vice-president of the World Bank. The Party has proposed that we promote balanced development among regions and among large, medium-sized and small cities and towns on the principle of balancing urban and rural development, ensuring rational distribution, saving land, providing a full range of functions and getting larger cities to help smaller ones, and thereby taking the path of urbanization with Chinese characteristics. Such a proposal represents the summarization of China's experience in the process of industrial and agricultural modernization over the past few decades and since the introduction of the reform and opening-up policies in particular, and also is an inevitable choice for China to change its growth model in the future.

Urbanization is an important social and economic phenomenon which has appeared since the Industrial Revolution and is relative to ruralization. In Western countries, "urbanization" means a process of significant social change in which a large section of the population migrates from rural areas to cities and small and medium-sized towns and transits from a self-sufficient small-scale production economy to a modern industrial economy including service industries in the process of industrialization. However, urbanization has a different meaning in China.

China has a huge amount of surplus rural labor, and it is impossible to transfer all these people to cities, as this would result in many new problems. The population of surplus rural labor in China now stands at 170 million to 200 million. There are 41 big cities in China with populations of over one million each. The populations of metropolises like Beijing and Shanghai already exceed 10 million each or even reach 20 million. If all the newly-born population and population transferred from rural areas flooded into the big cities, there would be unbearable strains on land and water resources, finances, transportation, environmental protection, health, public security and other aspects. Therefore, the concept of "urbanization" now generally used in the Party's documents is often modified to refer to small and medium-sized towns. The urbanization rate in China reached 51.27 percent in 2011, being over 50 percent for the first time, and is expected to reach 60 percent or so by 2020. Today China is in the stage of rapid advance of industrialization and urbanization. In this sense, China must take the path of urbanization with Chinese characteristics which it has explored.

If China's population reaches 1.4 billion, to reach the level of urbanization of medium-developed countries in the middle of the 21st century, nearly one billion Chinese people will live in towns, and the urbanization rate will reach 70 percent. The key to the problem is whether it is reasonable for the non-agricultural population to be mainly concentrated in cities, or for small, medium-sized and large cities and small and medium-sized towns to jointly share the non-agricultural population.

Why should China keep to the path of urbanization with Chinese characteristics?

China is now striving to change its growth model and expand the role played by domestic demand in economic development. Taking a path of urbanization with Chinese characteristics has already become an important part of China's development strategies. As indicated by China's experience and lessons in its development and in particular rapid economic development over the past 30-odd years since the introduction of the reform and opening-up policies, it is difficult to accomplish rapid economic growth by simply relying on investment and exports. The successful experience of advanced countries is that industrialization and urbanization supplement each other. China's urbanization has lagged behind its industrialization, hampering the sustainable development of the economy. Therefore, since the 17th CPC National Congress, the CPC Central Committee has proposed that we must keep to the new path of industrialization with Chinese characteristics, pursue the policy of boosting domestic demand, particularly consumer demand, and propel the transition in the economic growth mode from relying mainly on investment and exports to relying on a properly coordinated combination of consumption, investment and exports.

Many scholars consider the hundreds of millions of farmers in China's rural areas to be the largest consumer group in China. However, consumption depends not only on the number of people but the people's spending power, which in turn depends on both residents' disposable income and way of consumption. The millions of farmers in rural areas — and in China's central and western areas in particular — have low disposable incomes due to backward agriculture and low profit margins for agricultural products as commodities. In particular, they have lived in self-sufficient or semi-self-sufficient social environments for a long time, largely different from urban residents who mainly depend on markets and consume fashionable products. Therefore, it is difficult for farmers to develop corresponding spending power. To really implement or realize the policy of "boosting domestic demand, particularly consumer demand," on the one hand, we must increase farmer's disposable incomes; and on the other, we must develop a group of small and medium-sized towns with balanced urban and rural development so that farmers will live in towns or in communities during the building of the new countryside and develop a new way of consumption. To keep to the path of urbanization with Chinese characteristics, we must constantly boost domestic demand while balancing urban and rural development.

The benefits of urbanization are embodied in both economic development and improvement in the quality of urban and rural residents, particularly farmers, which is a valuable foundation of human resources for China to adhere to scientific development and accelerate the change of its growth model. China has long been a major agricultural country, and farmers represent the main social group in China and are related to small production, including the small production of the natural and commodity economies. But since the introduction of the reform and opening-up policies Chinese farmers have gradually developed modern ideologies and awareness such as independent personality and awareness of independence, democratic spirit and sense of equality in the course of building the socialist market economy and particularly when they work or start businesses in cities. Farmers, in fact, are changing into modern citizens. We have witnessed this profound change in many of the advanced coastal areas.

What are the principles and requirements of the path of urbanization with Chinese characteristics?

As explicitly stated in the *Report to the 17th CPC National Congress*, taking the path of urbanization with Chinese characteristics, we will "promote the balanced development of large, medium-sized and small cities and towns on the principle of balancing urban and rural development, ensuring rational distribution, saving land, providing a full range of services and getting larger cities to help smaller ones." Such a principle and requirement reveal the connotation of the path of urbanization with Chinese characteristics and points out the direction of the path.

Importantly, to promote the balanced development of large, medium-sized and small cities and towns, we should neither unilaterally develop large cities or megalopolises nor unilaterally develop small towns or small and medium-sized cities. Certainly, Chinese path of urbanization differs from those in the developed Western countries and in other developing countries in the Third World. We know that the development of any town depends on industry. Generally speaking, small towns depend on rural industry, small and medium-sized cities on modern industry and the service industry, and large cities on modern industry and tertiary industry serving modern industry. Most rural surplus laborers only receive primary or secondary education, and thus consider rural industry in small towns as their first choice for employment. Therefore, small towns represent the starting point of urbanization with Chinese characteristics. However, this situation is constantly changing. Many migrant workers gradually move from small towns to small and medium-sized cities and then to large cities. The urbanization mechanism also determines that there is a large-scale opening system between urban and rural areas which allows factors of production to freely flow and recombine between urban and rural areas to maximize the benefits of such factors by comparing benefit advantages. The balanced development of large, medium-sized and small cities and towns should take into account the development background and characteristics of large, medium-sized and small cities and towns in different regions. Such characteristics indicate the importance of small towns, and suggest that developing small towns is the foundation for advancing the development of large, medium-sized and small cities.

China's urbanization has already entered a period of rapid development, but many complicated problems and misunderstandings exist in the process. We must comprehensively analyze and conscientiously solve the problems in China's urbanization process, creatively advance urbanization with Chinese characteristics and promote all-round economic and social development by respecting the basic laws of world urbanization and referring to successful experience of forerunner countries on the basis of China's realities.

Relationship Between Basic National Conditions of
   Contemporary China, Characteristics of Chinese
   Culture and China's Political and Cultural De-
   velopment
Socialist Path of Making Political Advance with
   Chinese Characteristics
Socialist Path of Promoting Cultural Advance with
   Chinese Characteristics
Path of China's Peaceful Development

Chinese Path:
Political and Cultural Development

To keep to the path of socialism with Chinese characteristics, we must take the Chinese path of economic and social development, and follow the socialist path of making political advance with Chinese characteristics, the socialist path of promoting cultural advance with Chinese characteristics and the path of peaceful development. It is also an important task to constantly enrich and develop the overall path of socialism with Chinese characteristics in the political and cultural fields.

Relationship Between Basic National Conditions of Contemporary China, Characteristics of Chinese Culture and China's Political and Cultural Development

"Only the one who wears the shoes knows whether they fit or not." Xi Jinping quoted this vivid proverb to indicate "only the people are most qualified to tell whether the development path of the country is suitable or not."[49] Many people worldwide follow what is happening in the development of China's democratic politics and culture. However, some of them do not quite know China's history and realities, but invariably comment on Chinese politics and culture and even rashly criticize China as a country of totalitarianism and despotism, based on their own political experience and values. With such a bias, it is difficult for them to come to objective conclusions and explain why so many great changes have taken to China since the introduction of the reform and opening-up policies.

To understand the Chinese path of political and cultural development, it is first necessary to know that the Party pursues the ideological line of seeking truth from facts, which requires us to proceed from reality, especially the basic condition that China is in the primary stage of socialism, and respect the characteristics of Chinese culture. With regard to political and cultural issues in particular, the Chinese nation replaced absolute monarchy with republicanism in the Revolution of 1911, introduced Western culture to overthrow "Confucianism" in the May 4th Movement of 1919 and launched a wide range of political movements and cultural criticism campaigns after the founding of New China in 1949. Based on these experiences, we realize it is more com-plicated to explore and keep to the Chinese development path in the political and cultural fields than in the economic and social fields, because we must consider the basic condition that China is and will be in the primary stage of socialism for a long time to come and meanwhile take into account the historical characteristics of Chinese culture.

For example, when exploring the Chinese path of political development in the political field, we know that replacing autocracy and centralization of state power with democracy is a historical progress. China has reached a consensus on democracy but needs to further discuss what kind of democracy is most conducive to the sustained and sound development of China.

For many years, some people in Western countries have invariably told developing countries that they can enter the ranks of the advanced countries and change their backwardness as long as they adopted Western values such as freedom, democracy and human rights — the so-called "universal values", and establish an occidental competitive political party system and state system. However, the practice of world democratic politics has relentlessly told us that such a beautiful prediction has not come true; instead, social fragmentation, political turmoil, economic recession, war and slaughter frequently happen in many countries and regions under the pretext of "democracy." China's history of political development has taught us that we can neither address the issue by reaching a consensus on democracy nor build Chinese democratic politics by simply copying the democratic theory of Marxism or mechanically duplicating the forms of democracy of some developed countries. China is a large country with a population of 1.3 billion, so the Chinese, or even the world people will face a huge disaster if any such tragedy as happens in other countries or regions happens in China in the name of "democracy."

The Party members know very well their responsibilities, and persistently explore socialist democracy with Chinese characteristics that suits China's national conditions and cultural features, promotes the development of China's modern civilization and benefits all the Chinese people. For example, socialist democracy with Chinese characteristics has two forms, namely, electoral democracy and consultative democracy. Socialist democracy with Chinese characteristics is "characterized" by the combination of electoral democracy and consultative democracy.

Interestingly, such a "characteristic" was formed by history. Looking back on the founding history of New China in 1949, the Party originally planned to convene a political consultative conference together with other democratic parties to discuss a time for a general election, convene a people's congress and set up New China with people's democracy. For example, the Party's Central Committee called in a slogan published on April 30, 1948 for "all democratic parties, mass organizations and social elites to rapidly convene the political consultative conference, discuss and establish the people's congress and set up a democratic united government!"[50] Later, during the war of liberation the Kuomintang regime under the leadership of Chiang Kai-shek disintegrated, resulting in empty regions in many areas of China. At the same time, southwest China and southeast China were still war-torn and China did not have mature conditions for a nationwide general election. As a result, the Party and other democratic parties decided through democratic consultations to convene the extensively representative Chinese People's Political Consultative Conference (CPPCC) to exercise the power of the National People's Congress and set up the People's Republic of China.

We must pay attention to the following two points:

First, the CPPCC was convened because the Party and other democratic parties had already established a united front in the process of the Chinese revolution. The CPPCC is the organization of the unified front.

When the Party decided to found New China, Mao Zedong was wary of the slogan that "poor peasants and farm laborers should fight for and gain sovereignty," which appeared during the rural land reform in liberated areas, believing it to be a "left" slogan, and clearly pointed out that "in China, workers, farmers (including new rich peasants), independent industrialists and businessmen, small and medium-sized capitalists oppressed by reactionary forces, students, teachers, professors, ordinary intellectuals, (free-lance) professionals, open-minded gentlemen, ordinary civil servants as well as ethnic minorities and overseas Chinese should unite to fight for sovereignty under the leadership of the working class (the Party)."[51] Based on this guideline, the Party fiercely fought for national power and made great sacrifices for a new ruling system controlled by the people. Therefore, Mao Zedong proposed to build New China via the united front. As a result, the organizational form of the CPPCC was formed.

Second, the form of democratic consultation among all parties was implemented by means of the united front, so the CPPCC mainly exercises consultative democracy. In other words, New China was established in the democratic form of a state founding through consultation.

However, after the founding of New China and three years of national economic recovery, in November 1952 the CPC Central Committee decided that the conditions for a national general election of people's deputies were mature, and set about developing the Constitution and the Election Law, and prepared for the holding of the first National People's Congress. As a result, the CPPCC finished its task of exercising the power of the people's congress.

At that time, some non-communist party members worried that the CPC's decision would be unfavorable to some parties, classes and organizations which could not be selected from the general election. But Mao said at the Committee Meeting of the Central People's Government on January 13, 1953: "The government, based on the system of people's congresses, will remain the government of the united front of the people of all ethnic groups, all democratic classes, democratic parties and mass organizations, and will be favorable to all the Chinese people." During later elections of people's deputies, Mao and the Central Committee paid great attention to the proportion of non-communist party members and nonparty democrats among the deputies to the people's congresses at all levels. Nevertheless, some people were not elected people's deputies. In order to consolidate and develop the united front and encourage non-communist party members and nonparty democrats to give better play to their role of political consultation and participate in the administration and discussion of state affairs, Mao and the CPC Central Committee made a very important decision to continue to keep the organization of the CPPCC after the People's Congress was convened.

"The People's Congress is an organ of power, which will not hinder the establishment of the CPPCC for political consultation. It is of vital importance that leaders of all non-communist parties, ethnic groups and organizations consult on the major issues of New China. The draft of the Constitution has been completed through consultations and discussions. The People's Congress is of course extensively representative, but it cannot include all aspects, so the CPPCC is still necessary,"[52] said Mao when elaborating on why it was necessary for the CPPCC to continue to exist after the First National People's Congress (NPC) was convened on December 19, 1954. In other words, those elected as people's deputies might exercise their democratic rights in the People's Congress while those not elected might exercise their democratic rights in the CPPCC. Such a practice overcomes the contradiction between the "majority" and the "minority" in the elections in many countries, protecting the democratic rights of the minority while ensuring those of the majority.

From then on, the system of "Two Sessions" (NPC and CPPCC), which are convened every March in Beijing, was developed in China. The NPC mainly implements electoral democracy and the CPPCC, as an organization of the united front, mainly exercises consultative democracy, so two forms of electoral democracy and consultative democracy have been developed in China, which are remarkable masterpieces created by the Party's first generation of collective leadership with Mao Zedong at the core.

By further researching the history of the development of Chinese politics, we notice that in the later period of primitive society in China, a form of consultative democracy different from the electoral democracy of ancient Greek was implemented for handling political affairs, including changeover of power.

As recorded in the *Book of History*, Emperors Yao and Shun called "four tribal chiefs" or "12 prefectural governors" and "government officials of four slave-owning societies" to discuss public affairs, which were actually meetings of tribal chiefs. All important issues were decided by tribal leaders such as

Yao and Shun and tribal chieftains through consultation, and consultative democracy rather than electoral election (voting) democracy was practiced. "Selection" was a word also used in the ancient Chinese classics, as in "select the sage and the capable." However, "selection" is not "election." Shun was chosen as tribal leader by his predecessor Yao through consultations with other tribal chiefs at the "four tribal chiefs" meeting, which is recorded in the *Book of History*. Ancient Chinese called such selection of leaders "abdication." The word *xuan* in Chinese has two different meanings — election and selection. The way of election is voting and the way of selection is consultation, which are two different forms of democracy. Due to the philosophical concept of "harmony in diversity" that China has pursued for thousands of years, the Chinese people are more accustomed to the harmonious form of consultative democracy than to competitive democracy. Therefore, consultative democracy suits China's reality and has a profound cultural origin.

We should be aware that electoral democracy and consultative democracy are both limited when it comes to realizing democratic politics. Many young people favor electoral democracy and competitive elections very much because it has significant advantages, enables all people to cast a vote in a public and competitive way, and embodies the basic spirit and general requirements of democracy. However, in such democracy the right of over 51 percent of the voters is realized by sacrificing that of 49 percent of the voters by following the majority rule. Can we keep the advantages and avoid the disadvantages of electoral democracy? We combine electoral democracy and consultative democracy to realize the right of over 51 percent of the people by election and that of the remaining people by consultative democracy, so the rights of more people are guaranteed. Of course this is only simple mathematical analysis and the actual conditions are not so simple. Moreover, some issues of consultative democracy also need to be researched. Consultative democracy appeared when primitive society disintegrated, which finally evolved into an autocratic system. Why? Because consultative democracy can be exploited by despotic dictatorship. Therefore, it is necessary to research both electoral democracy and consultative democracy, but combining these two forms of democracy helps citizens realize their democratic rights. Based on an objective analysis of the democratic form designed by the Party, we notice a system design characterized by a combination of electoral democracy and consultative democracy, which better embodies the spiritual essence and basic requirements of democracy and is conducive to the improvement and development of socialist democracy in China.

The CPPCC is an important form but not the only form of consultative democracy. Consultative democracy is extensively applied in China, including specific practices of community-level democratic discussion meetings, government hearings and democratic consultation for the selection of official candidates. The 18th CPC National Congress stated that to improve the system of socialist consultative democracy, on the one hand we should regard the CPPCC as a major channel for conducting consultative democracy, and on the other hand organs of state power, political parties and community-level social organizations should develop consultative democracy.

By analyzing the position, role and historical origin of consultative democracy in China we clearly see that it was not by chance that consultative democracy became an important form of socialist democracy in China. Undoubtedly, combining electoral democracy and consultative democracy to develop socialist democracy with Chinese characteristics represents the Party's great creation by applying the Marxist theory of democracy to China's reality.

We realize that to explore and keep to the Chinese path in the political and cultural fields, it is only by conscientiously researching China's realities and cultural features that we can find the socialist path of making political advance with Chinese characteristics and the socialist path of promoting cultural advance with Chinese characteristics — the paths that conform to the direction of human civilization and suit China's reality, and form the path of China's peaceful development on the basis of taking a holistic approach to both the international and domestic situations.

Socialist Path of Making Political Advance with Chinese Characteristics

As emphasized at the 18th CPC National Congress, "People's democracy is a brilliant banner that has always been held high by our Party. Since the policy of reform and opening-up was introduced we have reviewed our experience, both positive and negative, in developing socialist democracy, and reaffirmed that people's democracy is the life of socialism. We have ensured that all power of the state belongs to the people, and worked to steadily promote reform of the political structure. As a result, we have made major progress in developing socialist democracy, and opened up and kept to the socialist path of making political advance with Chinese characteristics, thus charting a correct course for achieving the most extensive people's democracy in China."[53]

All mistakes in economic development and social development made by the Party after China entered socialist society were related to absence of political democracy and shortcomings in the legal system. Therefore, after the Third Plenary Session of the 11th CPC Central Committee decided to shift the focus of the Party's work to economic development, Deng Xiaoping explicitly stated, "Democracy is an important condition for emancipating the mind," and "To guarantee people's demo-cracy, we must tighten up the legal system and make democracy system-based and law-based."[54] Later, he further reiterated, "While vigorously increasing the social productive forces, we must reform and improve the economic system and political system of socialism, and develop advanced socialist democracy and complete the socialist legal system."[55] In 1982 Deng Xiaoping proposed at the 12th CPC National Congress that we must "take our own path and build socialism with Chinese characteristics," and explicitly pointed out that our goals included "advanced democracy." [56]

When elaborating on the Party's basic program in the primary stage of socialism at the 15th CPC National Congress, based on the goal of making China a modern socialist country that is prosperous, strong, democratic and culturally advanced, Jiang Zemin further defined the nature of a socialist economy, politics and culture in the primary stage of socialism and explained how to develop such economy, politics and culture. He said, "To develop socialist politics with Chinese characteristics we must govern the country by law and develop socialist democratic politics under the leadership of the Party and based on the position of the people as masters of the country."[57] Jiang further put forward the topic that "we should unswervingly march along the Chinese path of political development" in a speech delivered at the Party School of the CPC Central Committee on May 31, 2002, prior to the 16th CPC National Congress.[58]

Based on long-term practice, exploration and theoretical research, Hu Jintao raised the complete scientific concept of "the path of political development under socialism with Chinese characteristics" at the 17th CPC National Congress. As he put it, "As an important part of the overall reform, political res-tructuring must be constantly deepened along with economic and social development to adapt to the growing enthusiasm of the people for participation in political affairs. We must keep to the path of political development under socialism with Chinese characteristics, and integrate the leadership of the Party, the position of the people as masters of the country, and the rule of law. We must uphold and improve the system of people's congresses, the system of multiparty cooperation and political consultation under the leadership of the CPC, the system of regional ethnic autonomy, and the system of self-governance at the primary level of society. All this will promote continuous self-improvement and development of the socialist political system."[59]

The connotations of the socialist path of making political

advance with Chinese characteristics as a socialist path taken by China in the process of development of Chinese democratic politics are related to and differ from those of the path of socialism with Chinese characteristics. To sum up, we must, under the leadership of the CPC and basing ourselves on China's realities, adhere to a correct political direction, actively yet prudently promote reform of the political structure commensurate with the socialist market economy, socialist advanced culture and socialist harmonious society, constantly push forward the self-improvement and development of the socialist political system, uphold and improve the system of people's congresses, the system of multiparty cooperation and political consultation under the leadership of the CPC, the system of regional ethnic autonomy, and the system of community-level self-governance, expand people's orderly participation in governance, and ensure the unity of the leadership of the Party, the position of the people as masters of the country, and law-based governance.

To really understand the origin and scientific connotation of the socialist path of making political advance with Chinese characteristics, we must understand the united front that took shape in the Chinese revolution and continues to play a role in the period of peaceful development. China was a semi-feudal and semi-colonial society in early modern times, and its social structure was always characterized by complicated diversification. The CPC, which led the Chinese revolution in the process of political development, was very good at analyzing changes to classes in various periods as well as changes to their political attitudes in the revolution, including changes in the political attitude of the Chinese bourgeoisie, and established the united front that united the majority of the revolutionary forces. A people's democratic dictatorship established when New China was founded in 1949 was the government of the united front with the Chinese working class, peasant class, urban petty bourgeoisie and national bourgeoisie as the "people." In China, anyone who does not know about the united front under the leadership of the CPC does not know Chinese politics. Only by understanding the united front under the leadership of the CPC can we really understand the socialist path of promoting political advance with Chinese characteristics.

We can draw two very important conclusions: First, the basic political systems that we established after the victory of the new democratic revolution are political systems with Chinese characteristics. Second, these political systems with Chinese characteristics provide an important precondition and lay an important political foundation for the long-term development of Chinese socialist democratic politics following the completion of socialist transformation.

To improve and develop the democratic political system, we

have proposed and promoted reform of the political structure in the reform and opening-up process over the past 30-odd years. Here I will talk about two cases.

The first case is the Wukan Incident that caused a sensation both at home and abroad. On September 21, 2011, over a thousand villagers in Wukan Village, Guangdong Province, marched on the local Lufeng city government, shouting slogans and carrying banners, to protest appropriation of local land, unfair elections of local officials and other problems. They clashed with police, drove out the members of the villagers' committee and set up road barriers to block off the village, attracting attention from both the Chinese and foreign media.

Zhu Mingguo, deputy secretary of the Guangdong Provincial Party Committee, came to the scene to resolve the Wukan Incident. On January 15 a local Party members' meeting was convened at which Lin Zulian, who had led the protest, was elected general secretary of the Village Party Committee, and Hong Ruichao, who had taken a leading part in the protest, became a member of electoral committee. On February 11 Wukan Village elected villager deputies by secret ballot and elected the leaders of seven villager groups. On March 3-4 the village elected seven members of the villagers' committee and seven representatives of the villager groups by secret ballot, and all organizers of the demonstration were elected members of the villagers' committee. The Wukan Accident calmed down in March 2013.

The system of self-governance of villagers in China originated in the early 1980s. As explicitly stipulated in the *Organic Law of the Villagers' Committees of the People's Republic of China*, the director, vice director and members of villagers' committees should be directly elected by the local villagers, and no organization or individual may appoint, designate or dismiss a member of a villagers' committee. However, members of villagers' committees in some areas were not elected in accordance with the law. At the time of the protest, no villagers' meeting or villagers' congress was convened in the Wukan Village for the general election of the villagers' committee.

As summarized by Wang Yang, the then secretary of the Guangdong Provincial Party Committee, for the Wukan Incident, the democratic election later held at Wukan was not an invention but was conducted in accordance with the *Organic Law of the Villagers' Committees of the People's Republic of China* and the *Measures for the Election of Villagers' Committees in Guangdong*. He also said, "We had an idea then of analyzing this typical case and summarizing the experience to promote the development of village-level organizations."

Actually, China has advanced community-level democracy in a down-to-earth manner over the past 10 years since the

16th CPC National Congress. As of the end of 2012, China had already completed general elections of 89,000 community committees and 590,000 villagers' committees, and the average voting participation rate of villagers' committees had reached over 95 percent. In particular, urban and rural communities under self-governance of citizens improved the system of democratic management and form of self-governance. A wide range of systems of democratic management such as "democratic discussion meetings," "residents discussion meetings" and "community dialogue meetings," and various forms of residents' self-governance including "self-governance by courtyard," "self-governance by entrance" and "self-governance by building" have translated democracy from a political principle into a form of realizing democracy that can be seen and used by the people in their daily life.

In the development process of community-level democracy, neighborhood committees, villagers' committees and other legal community-level self-governing organizations are develop-ing, and more than 700,000 registered and over one million unregistered social organizations of all types also play an important role in urban and rural democracy and legal system building.

The second case is the fulfillment of citizens' rights amidst the combination of electoral democracy with consultative democracy.

China entered the period of intensive general elections of provincial, municipal-, county-, and township-level party committees in 2011. The people are always concerned about the progress of electoral democracy. The most high-profile event before the 18th CPC National Congress was the competitive election of 13 members of the Standing Committee of the Jiangsu Provincial Party Committee, which was called an iconic event of intra-Party democracy.

Jiangsu Province was the first to implement the "open recommendation voting" for the election and appointment of chief Party and government officials in cities, marking a new step in making the election and official systems more democratic after numerous innovations such as open recommendation and open election as well as open recommendation and direct election in some areas. From mid-April 2011 to early May 2011 six department-level officials, including three new municipal Party secretaries and the three acting mayors of Wuxi, Nantong and Suqian in Jiangsu Province, were elected by "open recommendation voting" of two rounds of recommendations and competitive elections.

The first general elections of county- and township-level people's congresses after the completion of the newly revised Electoral Law were successively launched on a national scale from 2011. As of the end of December 2011, 19 provinces, autonomous regions and municipalities directly under the central government had held general elections, and the voting participation rate reached over 90 percent. The electoral committees generally organized meetings to introduce the candidates to the voters. To help the floating population take part in the voting, the electoral authorities of registered residences may issue certificates of voters' qualification for migrant workers; electoral authorities of present residence may contact the electoral authorities of voters' registered residence to confirm their voters' qualification. It is unnecessary to re-issue a certificate of voter's qualification for a migrant worker who participated in the general election of the previous people's congress in the place of residence after such participation is checked and registered.

China practices and develops democratic politics, and has accomplished a series of important steps and achievements in reforming the country's political structure. Such steps and achievements have profoundly changed Chinese society over the past 30-plus years. Those people who believe China has only reformed the economic structure and not the political structure have not seen these basic factors and cannot explain why citizens are allowed to freely develop in the market economy, and why a successful market system and economic development have emerged in a "highly centralized autocratic society." Therefore, to observe and research the characteristics and trends of China's reform of its political structure, we must objectively and comprehensively understand China's practices of reform based on its reality.

The 18th CPC National Congress put forward the following seven tasks for promoting the development of socialist democracy with Chinese characteristics and deepening the reform of the political structure: 1. Supporting and ensuring the exercise of state power by the people through people's congresses; 2. Improving the system of socialist consultative democracy; 3. Improving community-level democracy; 4. Promoting law-based governance of the country in an all-around way; 5. Deepening reform of the administrative system; 6. Improving the mechanism for conducting checks and monitoring the exercise of power; and 7. Consolidating and developing the broadest possible patriotic united front.

According to the requirements of the 18th CPC National Congress, we must conduct the following four combinations to finish the seven tasks:

1. Combining electoral democracy with consultative demo-cracy. On the one hand, we should support and ensure the exercise of state power by the people through people's congresses. We should make good use of legal procedures to turn the Party's propositions into the will of the state. We should support people's congresses and their standing committees in

fully playing their role as organs of state power, in exercising legislative, oversight, decision-making, and personnel appointment and dismissal powers in accordance with the law, in strengthening organization and coordination of legislative work, in stepping up their oversight of people's governments, courts and procuratorates, and in tightening examination and oversight of all government budgets and final accounts. The proportion of community-level deputies to people's congresses, particularly those elected from among workers, farmers and intellectuals on the frontlines of various fields of endeavor, should be raised, while that of deputies from among leading Party and government officials should be reduced. Deputy liaison offices should be established in people's congresses to improve the mechanism for deputies to maintain contact with the people. The organizational system for organs of state power should be improved. The age mix and professional capacity of the members of the standing committees and special committees of people's congresses should be improved, and the areas of their expertise widened. The proportion of the full-time members of these committees should be raised. Deputies to people's congresses and members of these committees should enhance their capability to perform their duties pursuant to law.

On the other hand, we must improve the system of socialist consultative democracy. We should improve its institutions and work mechanisms, and promote its extensive, multilevel and institutionalized development. Extensive consultations should be carried out on major issues relating to economic and social development as well as specific problems involving the people's immediate interests through organs of state power, committees of the Chinese People's Political Consultative Conference (CP-PCC), political parties, people's organizations and other channels to solicit a wide range of opinions, pool the wisdom of the people, increase consensus, and build up synergy. We should adhere to and improve the system of multiparty cooperation and political consultation under the leadership of the CPC and make the CPPCC serve as a major channel for conducting consultative democracy. The CPPCC should, focusing on the themes of unity and democracy, improve systems of political consultation, democratic oversight, and participation in the deliberation and administration of state affairs, and do a better job of coordinating relations, pooling strength and making proposals in the overall interests of the country. We should strengthen political consultation with non-communist parties and actively carry out democratic consultation at the community level. Political consultation should be a part of the decision-making process, and should be conducted before and during such a process so as to make democratic consultation more effective. We should conduct intensive consultations on special issues with those who work on these issues, with representatives from all sectors of society, and with the relevant government authorities on the handling of proposals, and consolidate and develop the most extensive patriotic united front.

2. Combining making innovations in social management with strengthening community-level democracy. While making innovations in social management, we should promote self-management, self-service, self-education and self-oversight by the people in exercising urban and rural community governance, in managing community-level public affairs, and in running public service programs. We should improve the mechanism for community-level self-governance under the leadership of community-level Party organizations to ensure it is full of vitality. We should broaden the scope and channels of such self-governance, and enrich its content and forms, with the focus on expanding orderly participation, promoting transparency in information, improving deliberation and consultation on public affairs, and strengthening oversight of the exercise of power, to ensure that the people have greater and more tangible democratic rights. We should improve the democratic management system in enterprises and public institutions with workers' congresses as its basic form, and protect workers' democratic rights to participate in management and conduct oversight. Community-level organizations of various types should also get involved in

the integration of government administration and community-level democracy.

3. Combining improving democracy with improving the legal system. We should be aware that modern democracy is system-based and law-based, and that the rule of law is the basic way for running the country. We should make laws in a scientific way, enforce them strictly, administer justice impartially, and ensure that everyone abides by the law. We must make sure that all are equal before the law and that laws are observed and strictly enforced, and that lawbreakers are prosecuted. We should improve the socialist system of laws with Chinese characteristics, strengthen legislation in key areas, and expand channels for people's orderly participation in the legislative process. We should exercise government administration in accordance with the law, and ensure that law enforcement is conducted in a strict, fair and civilized way in accordance with due procedures. We should continue to deepen reform of the judicial structure and ensure that judicial and procuratorial bodies independently and impartially exercise their respective powers pursuant to law. We should carry out intensive publicity and education about the law, foster the socialist spirit of the rule of law, and adopt the socialist concept of law-based governance. We should enhance the whole society's awareness of the need to study, respect, observe and apply the law. We should ensure that leading officials

are guided by law in both thinking and action in their effort to deepen reform, promote development, solve problems and maintain stability. As the Party leads the people in enacting the Constitution and laws, it must act within the scope prescribed by the Constitution and laws. No organization or individual has the privilege of overstepping the Constitution and laws, and no one in a position of power is allowed in any way to take his/her own words as the law, place his/her own authority above the law or abuse the law.

4. Combining deepening reform of the administrative system with improving the mechanism for conducting checks and monitoring the exercise of power. Reform of the administrative system is a necessary requirement for making the superstructure compatible with the economic base. To reach the goal of establishing a socialist administrative system with Chinese characteristics, we should separate government administration from the management of enterprises, state assets, public institutions and social organizations, and build a well-structured, clean and efficient service-oriented government that has scientifically defined functions and satisfies the people. We should deepen the reform of the system of administrative examination and approval, continue to streamline administration and delegate more power to lower levels, and make the government better perform its functions of creating a

favorable environment for development, providing quality public services, and maintaining social fairness and justice. We should steadily advance the reform to establish larger government departments and improve the division of functions among them. We should improve the structure of the administrative setup and geographical administrative divisions, experiment with placing counties and county-level cities directly under the jurisdiction of provincial governments where conditions permit, and deepen reform of the administrative system at the town and township level. We should exercise government administration in an innovative way, increase public trust in the government, and improve its competence so as to make the government performance-oriented. We should strictly control the size of government bodies, cut the numbers of their leading officials, and reduce their administrative costs. We should continue the reform of public institutions based on the classification of their functions. We should improve the mechanism for coordinating structural reforms and conduct major reforms in a holistic way according to an overall plan. Meanwhile, we should improve the mechanism for conducting checks and monitoring the exercise of power. To ensure the proper exercise of power, it is important to put power, Party and government operations and personnel management under institutional checks, and uphold the people's right to stay informed about, participate in, express views on, and oversee government operations. We should make sure that decision-making, executive and oversight powers check each other and function in concert, and that government bodies exercise their powers in accordance with statutory mandates and procedures. We should continue to conduct scientific, democratic and law-based decision-making, improve decision-making mechanisms and procedures, seek the advice of think tanks, and establish sound mechanisms for decision-making accountability and remedy. Whenever we make a decision involving the immediate interests of the people, we must solicit their views on it. We must not do anything that may harm the interests of the people, and must correct any action that causes damage to their interests. We should make the exercise of power more open and standardized, and increase the transparency of Party, government and judicial operations and official operations in other fields. We should improve the systems of inquiry, accountability, economic responsibility auditing, resignation and dismissal. We should tighten intra-Party supervision, democratic and legal oversight as well as oversight by means of public opinion to ensure that the people oversee the exercise of power and that power is exercised in a transparent manner.

Socialist Path of Promoting Cultural Advance with Chinese Characteristics

The Party has always attached importance to cultural development. "A surge of cultural development will inevitably come along with upcoming surge of economic development. The era in which the Chinese people were considered uncivilized is gone. We will appear in the world as a nation with advanced culture," said Mao Zedong when New China was founded.[60] Since the introduction of the policies of reform and opening-up, the Party has repeatedly stated that we must lay equal stress on both material progress and cultural progress in the process of socialist modernization by taking economic development as the central task. On this basis, at the Sixth Plenary Session of the 17th CPC National Congress, the Party, based on a holistic appraisal of the cause of socialism with Chinese characteristics, profoundly summarized our historical experience of cultural development, scientifically analyzed the current situation and raised the important task of taking the socialist path of promoting cultural advance with Chinese characteristics and striving to develop a strong socialist culture in China.

The Party has explored the path of China's cultural building and cultural development for a long time by convening three plenary sessions to specially research the issue of cultural development since the Third Plenary Session of the 11th CPC National Congress in 1978. The first one was the Sixth Plenary Session of the 12th CPC National Congress, at which the Party shifted the focus of work from class struggle to economic development, and discussed whether it should promote cultural progress while concentrating on developing the economy and making economic progress or whether it should only value education on science and technology and cultural development while ignoring ideological and moral education. The second one was the Sixth Plenary Session of the 14th CPC National Congress after the Party stood the test of domestic and foreign political fluctuations and set the goal of building a socialist market economy in economic system reform. The Party discussed how to overcome interference from left and right, and strengthened its confidence in taking the path of socialism with Chinese characteristics; and how to build ideology and culture that are suitable for a socialist market economy. The third one was the Sixth Plenary Session of the 17th CPC National Congress, held in the new situation in the 21st century. The Party discussed how to deepen cultural system reform, promote the balanced development of the culture industry, boost the development and prosperity of socialist culture; and how to develop national cultural soft power and develop a strong socialist culture in China along the path of peaceful development.

Culture is the bloodline of a nation, the spiritual home of the people and the spiritual banner of a political party. The CPC is a Marxist political party with high cultural self-awareness. It has always attached great importance to cultural development and fully applied culture to guide the direction of the country, unite fighting forces and drive development in the various historical periods of the revolution, construction and reform. As an important meeting at which the Party specially discussed ideological and cultural development for the third time since the introduction of the reform and opening-up policies, the Sixth Plenary Session of the 17th CPC National Congress raised the important topic of the "path of cultural development under socialism with Chinese characteristics" for the first time in the Party's history of ideological and cultural development. This path of cultural development intensively embodies China's long-term practices and experiences in cultural development under the leadership of the Party, profoundly reveals the law of cultural development in China, follows the development trends of the times in accordance with China's reality, and reflects the new requirements of the Party and country for cultural development.

To keep to the path of cultural development under socialism with Chinese characteristics, we should ponder deeply and research the scientific connotations of the path. As stated at the 18th CPC National Congress, "To develop a strong socialist culture in China, we must take the socialist path of promoting cultural advance with Chinese characteristics. We should adhere to the goal of serving the people and socialism, the policy of having a hundred flowers bloom and a hundred schools of thought contend, and the principle of maintaining close contact with reality, life and the people. We should fully promote socialist cultural and ethical progress and material progress, and develop a national, scientific and people-oriented socialist culture that embraces modernization, the world and the future."[61] The "direction," "policy," "principle," "requirement" and "goal" are scientific connotations of the path of cultural development which point the direction of China's cultural progress. This is the only correct way to develop socialist advanced culture and realize the prosperity of Chinese culture.

Today, China has already opened up the way of promoting cultural advance with Chinese characteristics and clearly set forth the goal of developing a strong socialist culture in China. To adhere to the path and realize the ambitious blueprint, we must increase our awareness of and confidence in Chinese culture, actively do a good job in all respects and drive the new surge of socialist cultural development. China was considered the "Sick man of East Asia" by Western powers in modern times because China lagged behind other countries in economic development, and the Chinese people did not develop a strong culture. As a result, Mao Zedong said when New China was founded: "The Chinese people became spiritually active rather than passive after they learned Marxism-Leninism. The era in which the Chinese people and Chinese culture were despised in the world modern history is over. The great and victorious Chinese people's liberation war and people's revolution revitalized and continues to revitalize the great culture of the Chinese people."[62] Being "spiritually active rather than passive" represents the awareness of and confidence in Chinese culture in today's world, when culture is an important factor of a country's core competitiveness and plays an indispensable role in building its comprehensive national strength. Along with deepening world multipolarization and economic globalization, advancing science and technology, increasing mutual integration between culture and economy, and politics, and closer relations between culture and science and technology, anyone who takes the commanding height of cultural development will have powerful cultural soft strength and be able to take an active part in fierce international competition. Therefore, the socialist path of promoting cultural advance with Chinese characteristics put forward by the Party embodies its awareness of and confidence in Chinese culture.

Meanwhile, we have noticed that the Sixth Plenary Session of the 16th CPC National Congress was the first important meeting convened by the CPC Central Committee to specially discuss cultural system reform and cultural development. The Decision on Several Important Issues on Deepening Cultural Restructuring and Promoting the Vigorous Development of Socialist Culture was a programmatic document guiding China's present and future cultural development.

First, we must profoundly understand the goal and policy of deepening cultural restructuring. As explicitly pointed out at the Sixth Plenary Session of the 17th CPC National Congress, the ambitious goal of deepening and promoting the vigorous development and prosperity of socialist culture is to develop a strong socialist culture in China. Developing a strong socialist culture clearly requires us to focus on promoting advanced socialist culture so that it will further prevail among the people, fully boost socialist cultural and ethical progress and material progress, sustainably stimulate the cultural creativity of the whole nation, enrich the people's cultural and social lives, better safeguard their basic cultural rights and interests, comprehensively upgrade the people's moral quality and scientific and cultural quality in the new situation, build a spiritual home shared by the whole Chinese nation and make greater contributions to progress in human civilization.

Based on the new requirement of building a moderately prosperous society in all respects, the plenary session also put forward six goals and five important guidelines for cultural reform and development by 2020 in order to lead the people to deepen cultural restructuring. For example, the first goal is "to significantly improve the quality of citizens" and the third guideline is "to train socialist citizens with lofty ideals, integrity, knowledge and a strong sense of discipline."

Meanwhile, we should properly understand the tasks and contents of cultural restructuring proposed at the Sixth Plenary Session of the 17th CPC National Congress. In summary, first, the session put forward corresponding goals, tasks, policies and management measures of nonprofit cultural programs and profitable cultural industry so as to realize balanced development. Second, we should deepen the reform of state-owned cultural units, complete a modern cultural market system, innovate a cultural management system and improve the policy guarantee mechanism. Third, we should introduce Chinese culture to the world arena and actively absorb the achievements of excellent foreign cultures. Fourth, we should build a large contingent of cultural professionals. In a word, we should increase our awareness of and confidence in Chinese culture, focus on improving the quality of the nation and developing noble characteristics, more vigorously promote cultural restructuring, make cultural creations in the pursuit of socialism with Chinese characteristics and enable the people to share the fruits of cultural development.

To keep to the socialist path of promoting cultural advance with Chinese characteristics, we must, in the final analysis, revitalize the great culture of the Chinese people, enhance our national cultural soft strength, let China have its voice heard in the pluralistic world and turn China — a time-honored ancient country rich in cultural resources — into a strong socialist cultural power. We should be keenly aware that we must exert great efforts in building cultural identity to enhance our national cultural soft strength. Developing a strong socialist culture in China does not mean we will be committed to internal cultural control and external cultural dominance. To promote cultural development in a pluralistic society and world, we must respect the characteristics and reality of "pluralism," and make greater efforts in building cultural identity. In other words, for domestic cultural development we must enhance the identification of socialism with Chinese characteristics among the people and strengthen national cohesion based on such conscientious identification. For foreign cultural exchanges, we must enhance the recognition of Chinese culture among the people of all countries, and boost the attraction, appeal and transmissibility of Chinese culture on such a basis of recognition. It is right to talk in ways that others can understand in foreign cultural exchanges. To this end, we must respect the speaking and hearing habits of the people of all countries, and more importantly we must consider how to make people of different cultural backgrounds and ways of thinking understand so as to recognize our ideas and culture. When we introduce Chinese culture to the world arena, we will face nearly six billion out of seven billion people worldwide who believe in different religions or cultures. We should conscientiously research which elements of Chinese culture resonate with their beliefs and related ideologies and ethics, which elements can be accepted and liked by people of different cultural and religious backgrounds in different countries and which elements can be echoed by most people in the world. It will be meaningless if we talk much about Chinese culture yet others are unwilling to listen to or can't understand what we say.

By purposefully realizing such an important and complicated issue, and making substantial progress in cultural identity we will not fall into the trap of "cultural conflict" when we enhance our national cultural soft strength and develop a strong socialist culture in China. Therefore, we must grasp the favorable opportunity when the international community has shown an increasing interest to know or study Oriental and Chinese culture, to enhance cooperation with leading cultural institutions abroad, continuously expand the channels for foreign cultural exchanges and further promote the spread of Chinese culture.

In short, we still face many tasks to keep to the socialist path of promoting cultural advance with Chinese characteristics and realize the ideal of a strong cultural power. To this end, promoting the formation of "cultural identity" is a necessary path for China to take to develop cultural advantages that are in line with its economic and social development and international standing, and enhance its national cultural soft strength.

Path of China's Peaceful Development

Keeping to the path of China's peaceful development is an important strategic task proposed by the CPC Central Committee which is of great significance in China's present and future as well as domestic governance and diplomacy. Researching and adhering to this strategic task is an important condition for fully adhering to the path of socialism with Chinese characteristics, ensuring that China always soberly responds to challenges and grasps opportunities in complicated situations.

This task was put forward to better make an overall plan for the domestic and international situations, answer and resolve world opinions such as "China Threat Theory" and "China Collapse Theory," and foster a favorable international environment for accomplishing the goal of "a moderately prosperous society." George Walker Bush once regarded China as America's strategic competitor in the early years after he was elected American

President. Before the September 11 Incident, in particular, there was a fierce debate between the Red Team and the Blue Team in the US on how to respond to China's rise. Some American politicians worried about China's rapid rise. Against such a background, the "China Threat Theory" and "China Collapse Theory" rise and fall continuously to question China's development trend of peaceful rise in the process of reform and opening-up.

For example, as stated by Richard Bernstein and Ross H. Munro in *The Coming Conflict with China*, (1) China, with the largest population in the world, is a "potential superpower"; (2) It will have the largest economy in the world in the near future; (3) It is accelerating its process of military modernization; (4) Its nationalist sentiment is rising; and (5) Dominating Asia is the goal that China is striving for, and China will inevitably dominate one side of the Pacific Ocean in next 10 or 20 years. The result will be a conflict and even a military confrontation between America and China. This is the origin of the "China Threat Theory" and "China Collapse Theory," which are very unfavorable for China to complete the task of building a moderately prosperous society in all respects. We should fully explain to the world our strategic path of "peaceful rise" and the significance of the new international political and economic order to all countries in the world. At the end of 2002, a Chinese delegation headed by Zheng

Bijian, former managing vice-president of the Party School of the CPC Central Committee, paid a visit to America and their report to the Central Committee attracted great attention from General Secretary Hu Jintao and the Central Committee. The report said that to address this issue we should clearly state to the international community our path of peaceful development and foster a favorable international environment for accomplishing the goal set forth at the 16th CPC National Congress.

Objectively speaking, the important strategic thought was proposed to better summarize the rich experience gained by the Party in blazing the path of socialism with Chinese characteristics since the introduction of the reform and opening-up policies based on the domestic and international situations. China worked with neighboring countries to put forward the Five Principles of Peaceful Coexistence soon after New China was founded. China has creatively blazed the trail of socialism with Chinese characteristics since the introduction of the reform and opening-up policies. The path of socialism with Chinese characteristics is a path of modernization which requires China to adhere to reform and opening wider to the outside, and can help China shake off poverty and backwardness, become a prosperous and strong country and peacefully coexist and seek common development with other countries. Marching along this path, China will inevitably become stronger and stronger instead of collapsing, and be better able to safeguard world peace instead of imposing a threat to the world. In particular, viewed against the backdrop of other countries' history of modernization, China has accomplished remarkable achievements in modernization in the past 30-odd years neither by colonial plunder like developed Western countries or by waging wars, nor has it upheld the concept of a "big socialist family" to serve modernization like the Soviet Union. Instead, China has become actively involved in economic globalization and independently promoted modernization, opening up a path of accomplishing Chinese modernization by peacefully making use of resources in the world market. This is important experience gained by the Party when opening the path of socialism with Chinese characteristics in the process of reform and opening-up, as well as the important content and feature of the path of socialism with Chinese characteristics. Therefore, to grasp the important period of strategic opportunities in the first two decades of the 21st century, we must profoundly research and comprehensively summarize our rich experience gained in practice.

From the perspective of the Party's basic theory, the important strategic thought was put forward to better comprehensively expound the theories of Marxism on national development and international relations based on the domestic and international situations. Mistakes made by the Soviet Union in building a socialist country have exerted adverse impacts on the world. What's more, the international hostile forces have always spared no effort to slander communist parties and communism, talking about dictatorship and autocracy, without democracy, freedom or human rights, and that dictatorship and autocracy will inevitably lead to corruption and war. Therefore, to respond to the "China Threat Theory" and "China Collapse Theory" we should explain China's development facts as well as Chinese cultural traditions and refute these ideological misunderstandings. The Party proposed the path of China's peaceful development based on the basic tenets of Marxism, which always safeguards world peace and opposes colonialism, plunder by war and hegemonic expansion. As Deng Xiaoping explicitly put it, we build socialism to develop the productive forces and safeguard peace. The theme of peace and development in today's world makes it more favorable for China to take the path of peaceful development. Therefore, the Central Committee called on us to research and publicize the path of China's peaceful development so as to handle the present-day international relations and international issues, change the bad image of communist parties and communism caused by mistakes made by the Communist Party of the Soviet Union, build a new image of communist parties and Marxism in the world and make the scientific theories of Marxism of the Communist Party of China on national development and international relations better known to the world.

From the perspective of China's history and cultural

traditions, the important strategic thought was proposed to better inherit, carry forward and spread the fine traditions of Chinese civilization. The Chinese nation is a peace-loving nation and has the fine traditions of "harmony is precious" and "do not do unto others what you would not like others do unto you." In the Ming Dynasty (1368-1644), when China had a powerful navy, Zheng He led expeditions to the West for the purposes of cementing peaceful relations by upholding good faith and building harmonious relations with the countries he reached instead of for the purposes of expanding territory and plundering world resources. But the Chinese nation was invaded and enslaved by Western powers in modern times, so it has an extreme aversion to war and plunder, and a profound appreciation of peaceful development. This is the important and profound historical and cultural reason why China can unswervingly take the path of peaceful development, as well as an important historical fact in making China known to the rest of the world.

The path of China's peaceful development comprises five interrelated highlights:

First, generally speaking, the path of China's peaceful development is a path to be taken in the development process of socialism with Chinese characteristics. It is essentially the path for China to accomplish modernization, namely the development path of taking economic development driven by reform and opening-up as the central task and striving to basically realize socialist modernization in the middle of the 21st century, as spelled out at the Third Plenary Session of the 11th CPC Central Committee.

Second, the path of China's peaceful development is a fundamental objective for 1.3-1.5 billion Chinese people to address the issue of the right to live and right to develop, and enable one quarter of the world's population to enjoy a rich and dignified life. This is a development path that is committed to self-development instead of external expansion or world hegemony.

Third, a significant characteristic of the path of China's peaceful development is that China seeks development by winning a peaceful international environment, and safeguards world peace through its development. This development path adheres to consistency between domestic and foreign policies. In its domestic policy, China adheres to the Scientific Outlook on Development, takes the interest relations of all stakeholders into account in the process of reform and opening-up, and is committed to building a harmonious socialist society. In its foreign policy, China holds high the banner of peace, development and cooperation, pursues an independent foreign policy of peace, and makes concerted efforts with the people of other countries as a steadfast force in maintaining world peace to build a harmonious world. In other words, the path of China's peaceful development is a path for the country to accomplish socialist modernization by pursuing the policies of domestic harmony and international peace.

Fourth, the essence of the path of China's peaceful development is to independently build socialism with Chinese characteristics in the process of getting involved in economic globalization and in the process of realizing mutually beneficial results in the international community. For this, China faces various domestic and foreign challenges. On the one hand, China should be bold in and good at grasping strategic opportunities and adhere to opening-up to the outside world to get from the world market capital, technology and resources, including energy, that China needs for its modernization instead of plundering the resources of other countries by means of overseas colonialism or a "big-family" division of labor. On the other hand, China also independently overcomes various difficulties encountered in its development instead of bothering others or making trouble for other countries.

Fifth, the most profound connotation of the path of China's peaceful development is the great rejuvenation of Chinese civilization amidst interaction with other civilizations. The process of China's peaceful development is actually a process of great rejuvenation of Chinese civilization in the first half of the 21st century. Such great rejuvenation happens amidst interactions with other civilizations in the process of opening up to the outside, not in a closed country.

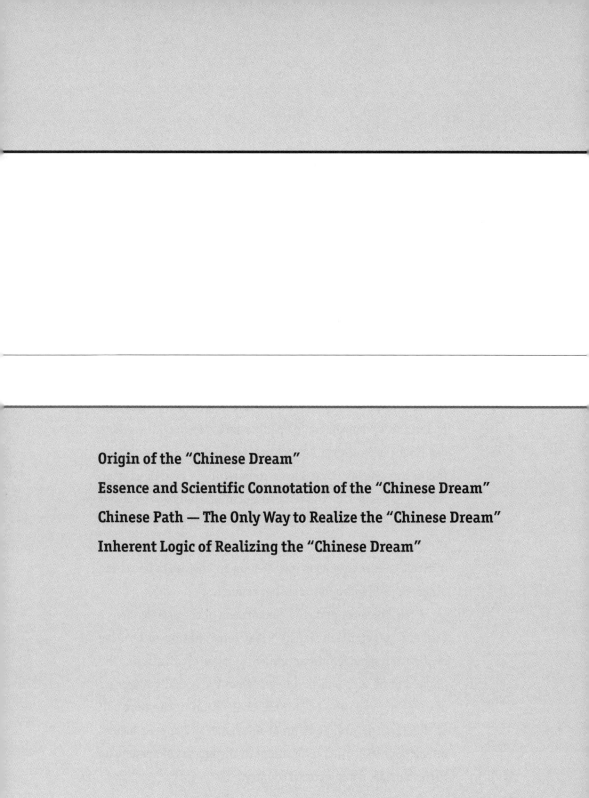

Origin of the "Chinese Dream"

Essence and Scientific Connotation of the "Chinese Dream"

Chinese Path — The Only Way to Realize the "Chinese Dream"

Inherent Logic of Realizing the "Chinese Dream"

"Chinese Dream" and Chinese Path

"Realizing the great rejuvenation of the Chinese nation is the greatest Chinese Dream of the Chinese nation in modern times," said General Secretary Xi Jinping after the 18th CPC National Congress.[63] He also comprehensively expounded on Chinese Dream and way to realize it at the closing meeting of the First Session of the 12th National People's Congress. These statements outlined the blueprint for the Chinese people to firmly march on the path of socialism with Chinese characteristics and strive to realize the Chinese Dream.

▌ Origin of the "Chinese Dream"

A dream is an ideal and a pursuit — a goal for the Party to mobilize the people, organize teams and lead the people to realize the ideal and pursuit step by step. It is the fruit of the Party's important experience in leading revolution, development and reform.

The CPC strives for communism, has a lofty ideal and is good at setting forth goals based on reality. In the period of the democratic revolution, Mao Zedong set the goal of "new democracy"; with the introduction of the reform and opening-up policies, Deng Xiaoping set the goal of "socialism with Chinese characteristics" and developed the three strategic steps of basically accomplishing modernization in the primary stage of socialism. Now, Xi Jinping has proposed the "Chinese Dream" by applying the spirit of the 18th CPC National Congress to mobilize the people.

The Chinese Dream has a profound background, historical connotations and historical requirements. In the prosperous reigns of emperors Kangxi and Qianlong in the Qing Dynasty (1644-1911), the Chinese nation arrogantly missed the opportunity of industrialization. After the Opium Wars in the mid-19th century, the Qing Dynasty was backward and was attacked by Western powers. As a result, China lost its sovereignty and was gradually reduced to a semi-colonial and semi-feudal country. From then on, seeking national independence and the people's liberation, and making China a prosperous country in which the people could lead a rich life became two important historical issues facing the Chinese nation. They gave rise to the dream of national rejuvenation that has been unswervingly pursued by the Chinese people generation after generation.

The path of realizing the dream is a long-term process of hardship. To realize the dream of rejuvenation of the Chinese nation, it is necessary to address the two historical issues, and fulfill the goals of achieving "national independence and people's liberation" and building a "prosperous and strong country and people's well-being." It will take the Chinese nation more than

200 years to realize its dream from the Opium War to the basic completion of modernization by 2050.

We realized the dream of "national independence and people's liberation" in the first 100 years. To realize the dream of rejuvenation of the Chinese nation, we had to address the first historical issue that the Chinese nation faced. The Chinese people made bold attempts — ranging from the Taiping Revolutionary Movement (1851-1864) under the leadership of Hong Xiuquan to the Hundred Days' Reform started by Kang Youwei and Liang Qichao in 1898, and then to the Revolution of 1911 under the leadership of Sun Yat-sen — to realize the dream of "national independence and people's liberation," but failed. The CPC, with Mao Zedong at the core and guided by Marxism, won the great victory of the New Democratic Revolution after 28 years of arduous struggles and helped "the Chinese people accounting for one quarter of the world population stand up." In other words, it took us more than one century to realize the dream of "national independence and people's liberation."

We will realize the dream of building a "prosperous and strong country and the people's well-being" in the second 100 years. Accomplishment of "national independence and people's liberation" created an indispensable political and social precondition for realizing the "greatest Chinese Dream" of national rejuvenation. China realized the historical transformation from new democracy

to socialism after seven years of profound social changes following the victory of the Chinese revolution. The Chinese people
embarked on the path of booming a prosperous and strong
country and well-being for all after China entered socialist society. China as a big Oriental country with a huge population
and a weak economic foundation made many detours because
it lacked experience in what kind of socialism it should build
and how to build it. The Third Plenary Session of the 11th CPC
Central Committee decided to shift the focus of the Party's work
and implement reform and opening-up policies. As a result,
China successfully blazed the trail of socialism with Chinese
characteristics and finally took the path of the great renewal of
the Chinese nation.

Based on the "three-step" strategy of Deng Xiaoping as well
as the strategic decision of "taking full advantage of the period
of important strategic opportunities in the first two decades
of the 21st century to build a moderately prosperous society in
all respects" made at the 16th CPC National Congress, we must
fulfill the two "100th-anniversary" historical missions to make
China a prosperous and strong country, achieve prosperity for
all and finally realize the "greatest Chinese Dream" of national
rejuvenation.

1   When we celebrate the 100th anniversary of the Communist Party of China we will have completed the building of a

moderately prosperous society in all respects and in the main achieve industrialization.

2   When we celebrate the 100th anniversary of the People's Republic of China we will have made China a modern socialist country that is prosperous, strong, democratic, culturally advanced and harmonious, and realize the great renewal of the Chinese nation.

Today we must work to realize the two "100th-anniversary dreams."

Now only eight years are left for us to fulfill the first "100th-anniversary" historical mission. In his *Report to the 18th CPC National Congress*, Xi Jinping said, "As I address you right now, we are convinced that, thanks to over 90 years of hard struggle, our Party has rallied and led the people of all ethnic groups of the country in turning the poor and backward old China into an increasingly prosperous and powerful new China, and opening up bright prospects for the great renewal of the Chinese nation. We are all the more proud of the historic achievements of the Party and the people, we are all the more firm in the ideals and convictions of the Party and the people, and we are all the more aware of the historic responsibility of the Party." As a result, the Party summoned at its 18th National Congress all the people to "Firmly March along the Path of Socialism with Chinese Characteristics and Strive to Complete the Building of a

Moderately Prosperous Society in All Respects." [64]

The Party Central Committee, with Xi Jinping as General Secretary, as stressed at the 18th CPC National Congress, is keenly aware of the heavy tasks and responsibilities on its shoulders, conscientiously undertakes the political responsibility to complete the building of a moderately prosperous society in all respects by 2020 and the historical mission of laying a solid foundation for the accomplishment of basic modernization by 2050, and summons all Party members and Chinese people to realize the "Chinese Dream."

Essence and Scientific Connotation of the "Chinese Dream"

Based on its historical origin, we have noticed that the "Chinese Dream" is a scientific pursuit with rich connotations and strong appeal. As Xi Jinping explicitly put it, "In the new historical period, the essence of the Chinese Dream is a prosperous country, national revitalization and the people's well-being. Our goal is to double 2010's GDP and per capita income for both urban and rural residents by 2020, and build a moderately prosperous society in all respects. By the middle of the 21st century we will have made China a modern socialist country that is prosperous, strong, democratic, culturally advanced and harmonious, and realize the great renewal of the Chinese nation."[65]

The essence of the "Chinese Dream" is its fundamental connotations. Broadly speaking, the Chinese Dream has specific and rich connotations:

First, the "Chinese Dream" belongs to the past, the present and the future. It is a goal of struggle put forward by the CPC that is part of the Chinese nation to realize its great renewal. The Chinese Dream reflects, in vivid language and with strong national sentiments, the requirements of two progressive ideological trends — patriotism and socialism — that are closely integrated in Chinese society in modern times. It crystallizes the lofty ideals of patriots in modern times, the pursuits of contemporary China and China's future directions, and represents a dream of "national rejuvenation" that connects China's past, present and future.

Second, the "Chinese Dream" has been put forward by the Party for it to undertake responsibilities for the country, the nation and the people. The "Chinese Dream" proposed by Xi Jinping shows the Party's strong sense of responsibilities, and represents the Party's lofty pursuit of benefiting the country, the nation and the people. By accomplishing the goal of building a moderately prosperous society in all respects and making China a modern socialist country that is prosperous, strong, democratic, culturally advanced and harmonious, and realizing the Chinese Dream of the great rejuvenation of the Chinese nation, we will build a prosperous country, and achieve national revitalization and the people's well-being, as profoundly stated by Xi Jinping at the closing meeting of the First Session of the 12th National People's Congress, when he comprehensively expounded on the connotations of the "Chinese Dream" as well as the path, spirit and forces necessary to realize the dream. This statement incisively reveals the significance of the Chinese Dream to the country, the nation and the people, and demonstrates the Party's conscientious undertaking of its responsibilities for the country, the nation and the people. Therefore, the "Chinese Dream" requires all Party members to adhere to the essential principle that "the Communist Party of China is the vanguard of the Chinese working class, the Chinese people and the Chinese nation," uphold the fundamental purpose of "serving the people wholeheartedly," and fully dedicate themselves to the task of building a prosperous country and achieving national rejuvenation and the people's well-being.

Third, the "Chinese Dream" belongs to the country, the nation and all Chinese people. "In the final analysis, it is the dream of the people. We must realize that dream by closely relying on the people and constantly bringing benefits to the people,"[66] said Xi Jinping. The Chinese Dream is the dream of a prosperous and strong country, and more importantly, the expectation and aspiration that are directly related to individuals' wishes, including housing, security of employment, social security and a beautiful living environment. Therefore, when talking about the "dream of the people" in his speech delivered on May 4, 2013, Xi stressed, "The people's well-being relies on the strength of the country and prosperity of the nation" and "Only when all individuals strive for the beautiful dream can we bring together powerful forces to realize the Chinese Dream." When stressing that the Chinese Dream is the dream of the people, Xi also emphasized, "The Chinese Dream belongs to us, and more importantly, to the younger generation. The great renewal of the Chinese nation will come true in the days of the coming of age of the younger generation." [67]

Fourth, the Chinese Dream belongs to the Chinese people, but it is also connected to the dreams of people all over the world. By realizing the Chinese Dream we will help to bring peace rather than turmoil to the world, and this represents an opportunity rather than a threat. China was invaded and oppressed by great powers, and knows very well the sufferings of a nation being bullied and without dignity. As an old Chinese saying goes, "Do not do unto others what you would not like others do unto you." The Party pointed out a long time ago that China will unswervingly follow the path of peaceful development and firmly pursue an open strategy of mutual benefits. Xi Jinping said when he visited the USA: "By means of the Chinese Dream, we seek to have economic prosperity, national rejuvenation and the people's well-being. The Chinese Dream is about peace, development, cooperation and mutually beneficial results, and it is connected to the American Dream and the beautiful dreams of people all over the world." [68]

Chinese Path — The Only Way to Realize the "Chinese Dream"

Xi Jinping stressed that to realize the Chinese Dream we must keep to the Chinese path, carry forward the Chinese spirit and mobilize the Chinese force. The Chinese Path embodies the Chinese spirit, namely the national character with patriotism at the core and the underlying trend of the times with reform and innovation at the core, and includes the Chinese force, namely the force of the unity of the Chinese people of all ethnic groups and the force of China in the course of reform and opening-up. Therefore, whether we can unswervingly keep to the Chinese Path is directly connected with the realization of the Chinese Dream.

Taking the Chinese path is keeping to the path of socialism with Chinese characteristics, which is the only correct way to realize the Chinese Dream. Xi Jinping said, "This path is hard-won. It has been opened up in the course of the great practice over the 30-plus years of reform and opening-up, in continuous explorations over 60-plus years since the founding of the People's Republic of China, in profound summarizations of the development process of the Chinese nation over 170-plus years in modern history, and in continuation of the 5,000-plus-year civilization of the Chinese nation, and thus has a profound historical origin and an extensive realistic foundation."[69] He added that we must cherish and be confident in the path that we have found from long-term arduous practice and summarization of historical experience. We know we will encounter many difficulties, challenges and tests in the historical process of realizing the Chinese Dream, but we are fearless and able to unswervingly take and constantly expand the path of socialism with Chinese characteristics instead of following the old path of lockstep or the erroneous path of direction change.

Taking the Chinese path means keeping to the path of reform and opening-up. The path of socialism with Chinese characteristics features reform and opening-up. Looking back on history, we realized the first 100-year dream of "national rejuvenation and people's liberation" by the people's revolution under the leadership of the Party. And we will realize the second 100-year dream of becoming a "prosperous and strong country and achieving the people's well-being" by reform and opening-up under the leadership of the Party. In the new period of socialist modernization development we frequently say that the Four Cardinal Principles are the very foundation for building our country, and reform and opening-up is the path to a stronger China, which is the most authoritative conclusion from practice. Today we must rely on reform and opening-up to fulfill the two 100th-anniversary historical tasks and finally realize the Chinese Dream. We will never deviate from this line. As Deng Xiaoping clearly put it, "After the Third Plenary Session of the 11th CPC Central Committee, we will concentrate on the four modernizations and focus on revitalizing the Chinese nation." Only by adhering to the basic socialist system, removing various institutional barriers in the way of national rejuvenation and fundamentally reforming the economic systems and other systems that are not suitable for the development of the productive forces can we realize the Chinese Dream of national rejuvenation so as to build, consolidate and develop socialism in China — a large Oriental country that has a large population, a weak economic foundation and a tortuous history. Practice has taught us that China has depended on reform and opening-up to shake off the Soviet model and develop into the second-largest economy in the world in a matter of only 30-odd years. We know that the socialist system with Chinese characteristics that we have created over the past three decades or so has distinctive features and high efficiency, but it is by no means perfect, mature and completed, so we must continue to deepen the reform and opening up. We are also aware that China now faces many contradictions, risks and challenges. In particular, it needs to further address many difficulties concerning the people's well-being, which can be overcome only by reform and opening-up.

Inherent Logic of Realizing the "Chinese Dream"

Regarding the relationship between reform and opening-up and the Chinese Dream, we should profoundly ponder and research the inherent logic of realizing the Chinese Dream, and correctly understand a series of complicated contradictions in the process of reform and opening-up. The Chinese Dream connects China's historical pursuits in the past, present and future, and the lofty pursuits of benefiting the country, the nation and the people. To realize the Chinese Dream we must follow objective historical dialectics to strike a dialectical balance between ideal and practice, between reform and development and between opportunity and challenge in the process of reform and opening-up.

First, the relationship between ideal and practice.

A dream is an ideal, but an ideal is not a daydream, and must avoid becoming a daydream, for which concrete action is needed. General Secretary Xi Jinping first warned us that "Making empty talk is harmful to the nation, while doing practical work can help it thrive" when he put forward the Chinese Dream. He added, "Everybody has his or her own ideal and pursuit as well as dream. Nowadays, everyone is talking about the 'Chinese Dream'. In my view, to realize the great renewal of the Chinese nation is the greatest dream for the Chinese nation in modern history. The Chinese Dream has concentrated the long-cherished aspirations of the Chinese people of several generations, represents the overall interests of the Chinese nation and Chinese people, and is the common expectation of every Chinese. History tells us that everybody's future and destiny are closely connected to those of the country and nation." Noting that the people's well-being relies on the strength of the country and prosperity of the nation, he said that "it is a glorious and difficult cause to realize the great rejuvenation of the Chinese nation, which calls for efforts by the Chinese people generation after generation. Making empty talk is harmful to the nation, while doing practical work can help it thrive. We, this generation of communists, must take what has been left to us by our predecessors as a basis for forging ahead into the future, and must build the Party well, unite all the Chinese people to build the country solidly and develop the nation in a bid to continue marching boldly toward the goal of the great renewal of the Chinese nation."[70]

"Making empty talk is harmful to the nation, while doing practical work can help it thrive" is an important conclusion for ruling the state and handling political affairs, summarizing thousands of years of historical experience and lessons. For example, General Zhao Kuo in the Warring States Period (475-221 BC) was only an armchair strategist, and his advice led to the destruction of 400,000 of his state's soldiers and the demise of the state of Zhao itself. Leading scholars of the Wei and Jin Dynasty period (220-420) were criticized by Wang Xizhi (321-379), a well-known calligrapher, for their "empty talk." Gu Yanwu (1613-1682), a noted philologist and geographer, summarized this lesson of history by saying, "Empty talk is harmful to the nation." General Secretary Xi Jinping is very familiar with these historical allusions and experiences, and exhorted us to keep in mind these examples on many occasions. He further connected the lesson with the Chinese Dream in a thought-provoking way during his visit to exhibition titled The Road Toward Renewal. Ideal and action are a unity of opposites, so it is necessary to correctly understand and handle the dialectical relationship between the two. The Chinese Dream is a rational idea based on reality and practice. Our ideal must be based on reality, come from practice, be applied to practice and conscientiously accept the test of practice. The Chinese Dream is our ideal, the aspiration and motive power of "action." It can come true only by means of action. To correctly understand and handle the dialectical relationship between "ideal" and "reality" as well as between "ideal" and "action," we must follow the dialectical logic of ideal and action.

Historical experience tells us we should describe the beautiful blueprint to the people and look into development prospects for the purpose of enhancing the people's confidence in socialism with Chinese characteristics. However, we should not set unrealistic expectations for the people, nor put forward slogans that meet the Party's ideal but cannot be turned into reality at the present stage. In other words, the Chinese Dream is a scientific ideal based on practice and will come true to life only by persistent action.

Second, the relationship between reform and development.

The most important action is to conduct reform and seek development in a down-to-earth manner. How can we strike a balance between reform and development? We will find no way out without reform, but must conduct reform in an orderly way. Neither should we conduct reform for the sake of reform, nor advance reform without considering the tasks and requirements of development. As we said, reform is the driving force, development is the goal and stability is the precondition — this indicates the relationship between reform and development. Over the past 30-plus years of reform and opening-up we have gathered rich experience, most importantly the experience that we must advance reform based on the reality that China is in the primary stage of socialism, aiming to overcome difficulties in development and find forms of building the economic and other systems that suit China's national conditions in a down-to-earth way.

Third, the relationship between opportunity and challenge.

Promoting reform means correctly analyzing the domestic and international situations that we face, boldly grasp opportunities and actively respond to challenges. As pointed out at the 16th CPC National Congress, we must seize tightly the important strategic opportunities to build a well-off society in an all-round way in the first two decades of the 21st century. However, opportunities always coexist with challenges. As a matter of fact, the process of grasping opportunities is invariably a process of standing up to various challenges and tests. Therefore, when deepening reform and opening-up and realizing the Chinese Dream, we must correctly handle the relationship between opportunity and challenge. It is of vital importance to propose and understand this issue in today's domestic and international situations.

To sum up, to realize the Chinese Dream, we should, as required by the *Report to the 18th CPC National Congress*, make "completing the building of a moderately prosperous society in all respects" and "deepening reform and opening-up in an all-round way" a united goal, follow the inherent logic of reform and opening-up and realize the dream of national rejuvenation in this process.

Notes

[1] Mao Zedong, "Analysis of the Various Social Classes in China," *Selected Works of Mao Zedong*, Volume I, People's Publishing House, 1991, p3.

[2] Hu Jintao, *Firmly March Along the Path of Socialism with Chinese Characteristics and Strive to Complete the Building of a Moderately Prosperous Society in All Respects—Report to the 18th National Congress of the Communist Party of China*, People's Publishing House, 2012, p10.

[3] Ibid., p1.

[4] "Tao" in Chinese is a synonym for "*lu*" (road). If the "*tao*" of "*taolu*" is explained as "*lu*," the two words are synonymous. "*Taolu*" should mean a "path" based on the Tao.

[5] Li Junru, *Proceed from the New Historical Starting Point—On the Scientific Outlook on Development*, Shanghai People's Publishing House, 2012, Title page.

[6] I discuss the basic thought of the "Tao" in Chinese culture as well as the relationship between the "Tao" and "path" in the hope that more people will understand the profound thinking and significance of the issue of the Tao and path

in Chinese culture rather than in the hope of changing conventional translations.

[7]   Xi Jinping, "Speech during a visit to the Road Toward Renewal exhibition, " *People's Daily*, November 30, 2012.

[8]   Xi Jinping, "Speech at the First Session of the 12th National People's Congress," *People's Daily*, March 18, 2013.

[9]   Ibid.

[10] The Four Cardinal Principles were proposed by Deng Xiaoping: Adhering to the socialist road, the people's democratic dictatorship, the leadership of the Communist Party of China (CPC), and Mao Zedong Thought and Marxism-Leninism. The Four Cardinal Principles constitute the foundation on which the CPC builds the country.

[11] Deng Xiaoping, "Implement the Open-door Policy and Learn World-advanced Science and Technology," *Selected Works of Deng Xiaoping*, Volume II, People's Publishing House, 1994, p133.

[12] Deng Xiaoping, "Several Opinions on Economic Work," *Selected Works of Deng Xiaoping*, Volume II, People's Publishing House, 1994, p198.

[13] Deng Xiaoping, "Hold High the Banner of Mao Zedong Thought and Adhere to the Principle of Seeking Truth from Facts," *Selected Works of Deng Xiaoping*, Volume II, People's Publishing House, 1994, p127.

[14] "On Socialism with Chinese Characteristics by Jiang Zemin" (Special Extracts), Central Literature Publishing House, 2002, pp519-520.

[15] "Decisions of the Central Committee of the Communist Party of China on Several Historical Issues Since the Founding of New China," *Selected Important Documents Since the Third Plenary Session of the 11th Central Committee of the Communist Party of China*, Volume II, People's Publishing House, 1982, pp839-844.

[16] Deng Xiaoping, "Opening Speech at the 12th National Congress of the Communist Party of China," *Selected Works of Deng Xiaoping*, Volume III, People's Publishing House, 1993, pp2-3.

[17] Hu Jintao, "Speech at the Seminar on Learning and Applying the Spirit of the 17th National Congress of the Communist Party of China by New Members and Alternate Members of the Central Committee," *Selected Important Documents Since the 17th National Congress of the Communist Party of China*, Volume I, Central Literature Publishing House, 2009, p97.

[18] Hu Jintao. *Firmly March Along the Path of Socialism with Chinese Characteristics and Strive to Complete the Building of a Moderately Prosperous Society in All Respects—Report to the 18th National Congress of the Communist Party of China*, People's Publishing House, 2012, pp10-12.

[19] Xi Jinping, "Speech at the Seminar on Learning and Applying the Spirit of the 18th National Congress of the Communist Party of China by Members and Alternate Members of the Central Committee," *People's Daily*, January 5, 2013.

[20] Wu Lengxi, *On 10-year Controversy*, Volume I, Central Literature Publishing House, 1999, pp23-24.

[21] Mao Zedong, "On the Ten Major Relationships," *Selected Works of Mao Zedong,* Volume II, People's Publishing House, 1986, pp720-721.

[22] Mao Zedong, "On the Correct Handling of Contradictions among the People," *Selected Works of Mao Zedong*, Volume VII, People's Publishing House, 1999, p214.

[23] "Annotations and Comments on Economics in the Transition Period by Nikolai Bukharin," *Collected Works of Lenin,* Volume 60, People's Publishing House, 1990, pp281-282.

[24] See note 21, p740.

[25] See note 21, p744.

[26] Mao Zedong, "The Situation in the Summer of 1957," *Manuscripts of Mao Zedong Since the Founding of New China,* Volume VIII, Central Literature Publishing House, 1998, p543.

[27] See note 15, pp839-844.

[28] Jiang Zemin, "Accelerate the Pace of Reform and Opening up and Automation, and Win a Greater Victory for Socialism

with Chinese Characteristics," *Selected Important Documents Since the 14th National Congress of the Communist Party of China*, Volume I, People's Publishing House, 1996, p10.

[29] "Communiqué of the Seventh Plenary Session of the 13th Central Committee of the Communist Party of China," *Selected Important Documents since the 13th National Congress of the Communist Party of China*, Volume II, People's Publishing House, 1991, p1422.

[30] Publicity Department of the Central Committee of the CPC, *Outline for Learning the Theories of Building Socialism with Chinese Characteristics of Deng Xiaoping*, Learning Publishing House, 1995, p21.

[31] "March Along the Path of Socialism with Chinese Characteristics," *Selected Important Documents Since the 13th National Congress of the Communist Party of China*, Volume I, People's Publishing House, 1991, pp56-57.

[32] Xi Jinping, "Speech at the First Collective Learning Seminar of the Political Bureau of the 18th CPC Central Committee," *People's Daily*, November 18, 2012.

[33] Ibid.

[34] The topic of the overall plan for the cause of socialism with Chinese characteristics was proposed by Hu Jintao. It was stated in the *Decision of the CPC Central Committee on Strengthening the Party's Governance Capacity* passed at the

Fourth Plenary Session of the 16th National Congress in September 2004 that the Party must improve its capability of controlling the socialist market economy, develop socialist democratic politics, foster socialist advanced culture, build a socialist harmonious society, and properly respond to international situations and handle international affairs. The Decision is a breakthrough in the traditional concept that society is made up of three elements, namely economy, politics and culture. As explicitly stated by Hu Jintao at the Special Seminar on Improving the Ability of Major Provincial and Ministerial Officials to Build a Harmonious Socialist Society held by the Party School of the CPC Central Committee on February 19, 2005, strengthening the building of a harmonious socialist society indicates that the overall plan for the cause of socialism with Chinese characteristics is composed of socialist economic, political, cultural and social progress. The Party expounded at the 17th National Congress the new requirement on realizing the goal of building a well-off society, and put forward new requirements for economic, political, cultural and social progress as well as "ecological progress." In the *Report to the 18th National Congress*, when elaborating on the path of socialism with Chinese characteristics, Hu Jintao further emphasized the joint importance of economic, political, cultural, social and ecological progress, indicating that the overall plan for the cause of socialism with Chinese characteristics had been further expanded into economic, political, cultural, social and ecological progress.

[35] Three-Step Development Strategy: Step One—to double the 1980 GNP and ensure that the people have enough food and clothing. This was attained by the end of the 1980s; Step Two—to quadruple the 1980 GNP by the end of the 20th century—achieved in 1995 ahead of schedule; Step Three—to increase the per capita GNP to the level of the medium-developed countries by the mid-21st century—at which point, the Chinese people would be fairly well-off and modernization would be basically realized.

[36] Three-Small-Step Development Goals: In the first decade, the gross national product would double that of the year 2000, the people would enjoy an even more comfortable life and a more-or-less ideal socialist market economy would have come into being. With the efforts to be made in another decade when the Party celebrates its centenary in 2021, the national economy would be more developed and the various systems would be further improved. By the middle of the 21st century when the People's Republic celebrates its centenary, the modernization program would have been accomplished by and large and China would have

become a prosperous, strong, democratic and culturally advanced socialist country.

[37] See note 19.

[38] See note 17, p99.

[39] *Advance Along the Road of Socialism with Chinese Characteristics—Report Delivered at the 13th National Congress of the Communist Party of China.*

[40] See note 2, pp20-21.

[41] See note 2, p22.

[42] Hu Jintao, "Speech at the 14th General Assembly of the Chinese Academy of Sciences and the 9th General Assembly of the Chinese Academy of Engineering," *Selected Important Documents Since the 17th National Congress of the Communist Party of China,* Central Literature Publishing House, 2009, pp501-503.

[43] "National Conference on Science and Technology Innovation Convened in Beijing," *People's Daily,* July 8, 2012.

[44] See note 22, pp240-241.

[45] Deng Xiaoping, "Adhere to the Four Cardinal Principles," *Selected Works of Deng Xiaoping,* Volume II, People's Publishing House, 1994, p163.

[46] Jiang Zemin, *Build a Well-off Society in an All-round Way and Create a New Situation in Building Socialism with Chinese Characteristics,* People's Publishing House, 2002, p21.

[47] Ibid., p19.

[48] *Collected Documents Since the 17th National Congress of the Communist Party of China,* People's Publishing House, 2007, p22.

[49] Xi Jinping, "Follow the Trend of the Advance of the Times, Promote Peaceful World Development," *People's Daily,* March 23, 2013.

[50] *Selected Important Documents of the Chinese People's Political Consultative Conference,* Volume I, Central Literature Publishing House and Chinese Literature & History Press, 2009, p1.

[51] Mao Zedong, "On Several Important Issues in the Party's Present Policies," *Selected Works of Mao Zedong,* Volume IV, People's Publishing House, 1991, p1268.

[52] *Biography of Mao Zedong (1949-1976),* Volume II, Central Literature Publishing House, 2003, p315.

[53] See note 2, p25.

[54] Deng Xiaoping, "Emancipate the Mind, Seek Truth from Facts and Unite as One in Looking to the Future," *Selected Works of Deng Xiaoping,* Volume II, People's Publishing House, 1994, pp144-146.

[55] Deng Xiaoping, "Congratulatory Speech at the Fourth Representative Assembly of Chinese Literature and Art Workers," *Selected Works of Deng Xiaoping,* Volume II,

People's Publishing House, 1994, p208.

[56] Deng Xiaoping, "Opening Speech at the 12th National Congress of the Communist Party of China," *Selected Works of Deng Xiaoping*, Volume III, People's Publishing House, 1993, p4.

[57] Jiang Zemin, "Hold High the Great Banner of Deng Xiaoping Theory for an All-round Advance of the Cause of Building Socialism With Chinese Characteristics into the 21st Century," *Selected Works of Jiang Zemin,* People's Publishing House, 2006, p17.

[58] Jiang Zemin, "Speech at the Commencement of Training for Provincial and Ministerial Officials of the Party School of the CPC Central Committee," *On Socialism with Chinese Characteristics by Jiang Zemin* (Special Extracts), Central Literature Publishing House, 2002, p304.

[59] Hu Jintao, "Firmly March Along the Path of Socialism with Chinese Characteristics and Strive to Complete the Building of a Moderately Prosperous Society in All Respects," *Selected Important Documents Since the 17th National Congress of the Communist Party of China*, Volume I, Central Literature Publishing House, 2009, p22.

[60] Mao Zedong, "The Chinese People Have Stood Up," *Selected Works of Mao Zedong*, Volume V, People's Publishing House, 1996, p345.

[61] See note 2, p31.

[62] Mao Zedong, "The Idealistic Viewpoint on History Is Bankrupt," *Selected Works of Mao Zedong*, Volume IV, People's Publishing House, 1991, p1516.

[63] See note 7.

[64] See note 2, pp1-2.

[65] "Xi Jinping Accepts Joint Written Interview Questions by Media of Three Latin American Countries," Xinhua News Agency, Beijing, May 31, 2013.

[66] Xi Jinping, "Speech at the Closing Meeting of the First Session of the 12th National People's Congress," *People's Daily*, March 18, 2013.

[67] Xi Jinping, "Speech at the Meeting with Excellent Young Representatives from All Circles," *People's Daily*, May 5, 2013.

[68] "Speech by Xi Jinping at a press conference together with President Obama," *People's Daily*, June 8, 2013.

[69] Xi Jinping, "Speech at the First Session of the 12th National People's Congress, " *People's Daily*, March 18, 2013.

[70] See note 7.

图书在版编目（CIP）数据

中国道路与中国梦：英文 ／ 李君如著.—北京：外文出版社，2013
ISBN 978-7-119-08600-2

Ⅰ.①中… Ⅱ.①李… Ⅲ.①国特色社会主义－社会主义建设模式－研究
－英文 Ⅳ.①D616

中国版本图书馆CIP数据核字(2013)第260259号

策　　划：徐　步
作　　者：李君如
统　　筹：解　琛
英文翻译：李花玉
英文审定：Paul White　郁　苓
责任编辑：文　芳
装帧设计：〓 设计·邱特聪
印刷监制：张国祥

中国道路与中国梦

李君如　著

出　版　人：徐　步
出版发行：外文出版社有限责任公司
地　　　址：北京市西城区百万庄大街24号　　邮政编码：100037
网　　　址：http://www.flp.com.cn　　　　　　电子邮箱：flp@cipg.org.cn
电　　　话：008610-68320579（总编室）　　008610-68996158（编辑部）
　　　　　　008610-68995852（发行部）　　008610-68996183（投稿电话）

印　　　刷：北京朝阳印刷厂有限责任公司
经　　　销：新华书店/外文书店
开　　　本：787×1092mm　1/16
字　　　数：200千
印　　　张：14.5
版　　　次：2014年3月第1版第1次印刷
书　　　号：ISBN 978-7-119-08600-2
定　　　价：98.00元